10638046

The
Magic
of
Goals

WESTERN IOWA TECH-LIBRARY

THE MAGIC OF GOALS

All Rights Reserved Including
The Right of Reproduction
In Whole Or In Part
And In Any Form Whatsoever

Copyright© 1979 By Ronald L. Reynolds

Published By
Discovery Publications
Laguna Hills, California

First Printing, April 1979
Second Printing, January 1980
Third Printing, May 1983
Fourth Printing, September, 1983

Library Of Congress Card Catalog Number
83-71017

ISBN Number
0-939490-01-3

Designed And Produced
By
Ronald L. Reynolds

Printed In The United States Of America

TO JACKIE — WHO TAUGHT ME OF MY VALUES, SHARED MY
     TROUBLES, AND HELPED ME TO UNDERSTAND THAT
     EVERYBODY NEEDS SOMEBODY ELSE.

TO MIKE, CHRIS, STEVE, SCOTT — AND CONNIE —
     WHO PAID THE PRICE, AND GAVE ME THE REASONS
     FOR BECOMING WHAT I AM BECOMING.

TO JIM ROHN — WHOSE WORDS AWAKENED A SPIRIT

TO BRUCE COLLARD AND DORE WACHTEL — WHO WILL KNOW WHY...

TO DIANE — WHO READ MY WRITING WHEN OTHERS COULDN'T.

TO JERRY PETERSON — WHOSE EXPERTISE WAS INVALUABLE.

TO THE PEOPLE, SITUATIONS, AND EVENTS THAT LET ME BE
AVERAGE. IT WASN'T YOU, IT WAS ME. THANK YOU FOR GIVING ME
A LIFE OF FAILURE AND DISAPPOINTMENT. IT HAS MADE ME
STAND ERECT.

The most exciting awareness of life lies in the knowledge that we can have more than we've got because we have the capacity of becoming more than we are.

The Magic of Goals

RONALD L. REYNOLDS

Some people manage to survive well into their thirties living a life of existence rather than a life of substance. Ron Reynolds was typical of that kind of person. He had married at eighteen, primarily to escape an unhappy home life. By the time he was twenty-two he and his wife had four children. To support them, he took a job in aerospace at a small rocket development laboratory in the mountains of West Virginia. He found his electronic technician responsibilities dull and the pay inadequate. With a family, however, he could not afford to risk trying something else.

One day in early 1968 during a coffee break — those fifteen minute periods when people discuss politics, incompetent supervision, and the unfairness of the pay schedule — Reynolds heard someone say that "money" was in sales. By October of that year, his disenchantment with his direction and his deteriorating financial situation became so severe that he resigned his position and moved to Washington, D.C. where he began a sales career selling life insurance. While his income and self-satisfaction improved, his confidence that he had found his "chosen career" did not. For the next several years Ron Reynolds tried four different sales positions, doing fairly well in each, but discovering that there had to be more to life than just earning a living.

Finally, a business position brought him and his family to California. The new environment, the apparent "unlimited opportunity" of his new sales management position and his new income made the future appear to glow with excitement. Reynolds became an avid student of sales techniques, leadership qualities, and people. He attended nearly every seminar available to increase his ability as a sales professional. Suddenly, the company which had brought so much promise to his life collapsed, and he found himself living on the limited savings which his short-lived success had provided. To make things smoother, his wife went to work selling shoes. His dream shattered and his confidence shaken, Reynolds went into a mental tailspin, and his troubles were just beginning. Problems developed with his children — a new experience for this close family that had survived the frequent challenges of a growing family.

For a period of six months, a series of incredible events took place. As a consequence, the solid, twenty-year marriage ended in divorce with Reynolds shaken, alone, and broke.

Opportunity has a unique way of presenting itself — often in disguise and at a time when we are least likely to recognize it. Ron Reynolds found himself sitting alone at the South Coast Plaza Hotel in Orange County, California. He was thumbing through the *Los Angeles Times*, vainly trying to match available jobs with his deteriorating skills. Through the revolving door and into the lobby entered Mr. E. James Rohn, Chairman of the Board of Jim Rohn Productions, a man whose personal development seminar Reynolds had heard in Washington, D.C. several years before. It was that seminar that had had the greatest effect in turning Reynolds' sales career from mediocrity to high productivity. Reynolds immediately approached Rohn, and the two spent several hours together discussing life, business, and the personal dilemma which had consumed Reynolds.

As good fortune sometimes does, she smiled upon Ron Reynolds that day. Rohn had arrived in town to conduct his seminar — the same seminar that had taught Reynolds that "Successful living is an attitude" and that "What happens is not important — it's what you do about what happens that makes the difference." If there was one thing that he needed more than a job, Reynolds needed a new attitude — a new insight into dealing with both adversity and challenge, and a renewed confidence in himself and the abilities which lay sleeping within him.

With the reunion of these two men came not only the ideas and inspiration that Reynolds needed to hear, but an opportunity as well. Rohn was recruiting a sales staff to offer to the public his personal development package of seminars, tapes, workbooks, and workshops. Since first hearing Rohn, Ron Reynolds had dreamed of doing just that. In fact, after that first seminar in Washington he had approached Jim Rohn and announced, "Someday I will do what you do; in fact, someday I'm going to go to work with you!" And here was exactly what he needed — an opportunity to earn an income while selling a product designed to change human attitudes. His two greatest needs could be satisfied. And it would be the achievement of a dream and a goal which he had set several years before — to work with the man whose words had had such a major effect on his life.

For the next year, Reynolds fought against nearly constant adversity. The challenges in helping to build a new company were frequently awesome. The income was usually just enough for him to meet his minimum expenses. He rode buses to keep sales appointments and sometimes walked several miles to appear as a guest speaker at small service clubs. He often slept on the floor of the office from which he worked — a fourteenth floor suite across the street from the Los Angeles Marriott Hotel. Often he would sit alone at night and read, study, or reflect —and sometimes gaze across the street at the lavish Marriott and daydream about the food and the soft beds. He would watch the guests come and go. They seemed to be people living normal lives, surrounded by comfort and convenience, while he sat chilled, hungry, and alone waiting for the arrival of tomorrow — when he would once again swing his meager hatchet of effort at the mighty oak of challenge. Often his mind drifted to his family, and he remembered the happy years.

How could a man well into his middle years — with business experience, good health, love and loyalty for his family, and a willingness to work hard — come to such debasing circumstances? He had done poorly in high school, barely graduating. But in his twenties, while working full time and raising a family, he had gone to college at night and had maintained a "B" average. He was well read and communicated well, and had helped build several corporations with his ideas and insights. Yet here he was starting over; fighting to get off his mental and financial knees. And he continued to work on himself — his attitude, goals, and the better future he knew would come if he could only remember to work harder on himself than on anything else.

Finally, the breakthrough came! His sales increased and the company became a million dollar corporation. Reynolds had become a product of the product. His speeches touched people; and with every effort designed to help others, he found he was helping himself. He was soon made the personal representative of the Chairman of the Board. And then finally, two years after joining Rohn as a salesman, Reynolds was appointed to conduct the prestigious *Leadership Seminar* of Jim Rohn Productions, participating equally with Rohn, whose seminar ten years earlier had meant so much to him. He had reached a goal which had often seemed unreachable, and was now in demand as a speaker and a consultant.

From the loneliness of Suite 1422 overlooking the Marriott in Los Angeles, the endless bus trips, and the long walks across the San Fernando Valley, Ron Reynolds now found himself at the Hyatt Regency in San Francisco, the Acapulco Princess, and the Southern Sun in Johannesburg, South Africa. His better future is now, and it is just beginning. His message becomes stronger, and his confidence is supreme. There is magic in goals and Reynolds has proven it. He has discovered that sometimes agony must precede achievement. And for those who remember that, and work on developing and discovering their talents, the potential rewards are immeasurable.

This book was first printed in 1979, and is now in its fourth printing. In the four years that have elapsed since Mr. Reynolds' original writing of the manuscript, he has continued the momentum which began in 1976. He has, in the past four years, achieved even greater success through investing in real estate. In addition, he co-authored *The Seasons of Life* with E. James Rohn, and authored a workbook designed to supplement *The Magic of Goals* and to provide practical steps for converting the philosophy of goal-setting into practical reality.

Mr. Reynolds has been selected for inclusion in *Who's Who in Orange County* as well as *Who's Who in California*. He considers his greatest accomplishment to be his creation of *The Gift*, a novel scheduled for release in April of 1983 which took nearly two years to create. And, to give perhaps even greater credibility to the value of setting goals through using the insights included within these pages, Ron Reynolds became President and Chief Executive Officer of Jim Rohn Productions on December 8, 1982. Jim Rohn, the teacher, and Ron Reynolds, the student, now function together in sharing their message across America. Their enterprise has produced a variety of self-help tape programs, books, workbooks, seminars, and video seminars that bring their unique and life-changing message to all those who believe themselves to be worthy participants in the search for achievement.

"Somewhere out there are several million people who sit in their own Suite 1422," Reynolds says, "and words are the only way to touch them with hope and renewed ambition. Not just words, but words set on fire with the high intensity of emotion, and I want to help reach whoever wants to listen."

His speeches and seminars now end with the familiar *Irish Blessing*, and so should this brief sketch of the life of Ron Reynolds—

"May the road rise to meet you.
May the wind be always at your back.
May the sun shine warm on your face,
And the rain fall gently in your field,
And until we meet (again), may
God hold you softly in the palm of his hand."

The Magic of Goals

THE KEY TO BECOMING ALL YOU WERE INTENDED TO BE —

Too many of us move from the exciting anticipation of childhood to the memories of the aged with very little of substance in between.

1

The most frustrating thing for a person to experience is the intense desire for an above average income, an above average job, and an above average degree of happiness while knowing that his present personal circumstances will never allow his wish to be granted. In our contemporary society, we are continually confronted with the objects of the better life. Television, magazines, and all the tools of the media blast away at us, painting pictures of the better home, the new car, the easy loan, the magic credit card, and the king-size-living-color TV set. But only a handful of society can ever hope to possess these dream items, due to steadily increasing demands by taxes and the basic cost of staying alive. The frustration caused by the confrontation of objects, coupled with the inability to qualify financially for the possession of those objects produces a condition which psychologists call "Anomie." It simply means not being able to enjoy the rewards of the better life while being subjected to a daily "blitz" of appeals to buy the objects which provide those rewards. The media, to make matters worse, would subtly have us accept the fact that everyone else has one — whatever it is — and the feeling we get from being unable to join the crowd produces massive feelings of depression and inadequacy. Wives and husbands argue incessantly over not being able to keep up with the Joneses — or often go into such deep depression that they just simply don't bother arguing anymore because they don't bother talking anymore. All of these conditions and events are greatly complicated at the Christmas season, when we are expected to buy and share in even larger quantities, and our being unable to do so only complicates the dilemma further. "Tis the season to be jolly" turns into a veritable nightmare of commercials, unfulfilled promises, unanswered prayers, and excessive alcohol consumed by the hopeless and distraught in hopes that it will remove from their consciousness the painful reality of their constantly deteriorating and demeaning circumstances.

There is, however, an answer for changing human circumstances from mediocrity to abundance and prosperity. It will work for the poorly educated or the highly educated. It applies to, and serves well, men and women of all nations, races, and creeds. It is well understood by only a few, but its results are both incredible and highly predictable, if used. The answer is in learning the *meaning of setting goals!*

All of us are familiar with the word "goals." In fact, perhaps we are *too* familiar with the word. And when we become too familiar with anything we usually take it for granted, whether it be a unique love affair, an automobile, or our physical health. We have heard people, corporations, and governments refer to "goals" to such an extent that often we subconsciously relate its meaning to be something negative — something that *someone else* wants us to do that we really do not want for ourselves. When a corporation, for example, announces a goal, it seems that we all will have to make certain sacrifices. The goal seems to become a challenge, and people often resent being challenged. It is an intrusion upon our private right, and therefore has an automatically negative connotation. Perhaps this is why many people don't like hearing about the value of goal-setting as it applies to their personal and family lives: their past experience with the subject has been in some way negative.

There is, however, a significant difference between the goals someone else sets for us and the goals we set for ourselves. But whether we are seeking the goal we imposed on ourselves, or one imposed by someone else, one thing is for certain: either we set our own goals and plans, or we are going to find that we fit into the goals and plans of someone else. And if it is the latter, we may find out only too late that we do not particularly like what they have planned for us. Either way, we are all fitting into a plan of some kind. Someone's plan has us doing what we presently find ourselves doing as an occupation. Hopefully, that occupation is progressive enough to allow us to formulate our own individual plan — something that allows us to function almost as a company within a company, using our own God-given talents which result in profit both for the company and ourselves.

Let's briefly look at the magic of setting personal goals, and what they are really all about. First of all, be certain of one thing — the biggest reason that most people fail to do better in life is that they simply don't know what they want. As teenagers, none of us ever desired to be mediocre or average; we just assumed that we would automatically have an abundance of the finer things in life. How it would come about was not important — we just knew that it would. All we had to do was to enjoy ourselves and wait for adulthood to seize us, and success would surely be ours. Then along came the world's greatest love affair, followed by marriage, and followed not long after that by bills and responsibilities. Then came the children, and even greater responsibilities. More often than not, our occupation by this time was not one of our own choosing — certainly not the fulfillment of a life-long dream. It was, at best, a fairly good-paying and secure "job." The pay check was always there, and the benefit package was adequate, so we elected to stay; not because we wanted to, or because we were in love with our work, but because we had to, out of economic necessity. Some of us may have finally developed the courage to leave and accept a new job, usually because it paid more. Shortly we found that we didn't like it any better than the previous job, but we stayed. Eventually, we became lost, working not to achieve, but to survive. As one writer once put it, "Most people die at age thirty, but are not buried until age sixty."

The hopes and dreams of earlier years not only are unattained, they are even forgotten. Our high ambition dissolves into a life of existence rather than a life of substance. If the marriage survives at all, it is usually because of the children, and we continue along in this hopeless rut, walking that long, gray road of mediocrity — never really losing, but never winning either. Life becomes fairly dull, repetitive, and unchallenging, and we find ourselves spending most of our time looking forward to Friday and hating Monday; waiting for the kids to grow up; and then waiting for retirement; and then, waiting for the inevitable fulfillment of an uneventful life, with internment at 2 p.m. at the local cemetary.

If this sounds all too familiar, it could well be the result of the absence of any well-planned and consistently executed goals for living a better life. All of us need something in our lives that offers constant challenge, excitement, and the promise of the better future. No one knows us better than ourselves, therefore we must find out for *ourselves* what "turns us on." We must take the time to discover (perhaps *rediscover* is a better word, since all of us once had a dream) the things we want to have, become, see, read, visit, listen to, share, and get rid of. All of these are called "goals," and they begin to take shape not when we simply think about them, but when we take the time to physically put them on paper.

And there is one of the keys towards making goals work for us!

For goals to become part of us and work for us, they must be written on paper, not kept in the mind. Left in the mind, they remain too vague to ever be effective. When committed to writing, goals become incredibly specific, and the more detailed their description, the stronger becomes our desire to have them. Remember an earlier comment — most people don't know what they want! One of the major benefits of writing out goals is to force ourselves to rediscover what it is like to want something. In the beginning, the process comes along very slowly (which is a sure sign that we really don't know what we want). But as we force ourselves, new ideas spring forth, until at last we find ourselves unable to write fast enough.

The major ingredient to setting goals and making them work for you is the feeling that is generated deep inside — that driving force that tells us we are finally on the right course. It gets us out of bed earlier each morning and keeps us up a little later each night; it occasionally makes sleep difficult to find because the thoughts still linger about today (unlike the worries that used to keep us awake), and there is a near childlike excitement about what tomorrow may bring. It is this new feeling that makes us smile more, laugh louder, walk faster, and in all ways become more of all we have always wanted to be.

Unfortunately, this feeling cannot be taught —it is individual and must come from within each of us. One person cannot tell another how to get it; only the basic mechanics that cause it to happen can be passed from one to another. Also, each of us must be ready for it. On any given day we may find ourselves reading the proper book, receiving the exact instruction, or attending the seminar or training class that triggers others to go on to do well, but the books, seminars, or classes fail to do anything for *us*. We are all human and really want to do well. And yet sometimes when another person hears the same words we do, and goes into action and finds success, while we do not, it simply means we are not ready. Be sure of one thing, however — the book or seminar did not fail us, we failed ourselves. As one great man has said, "When the student is finally ready, the teacher will appear."

2

Here are those basic steps which, if followed, may well trigger that sleeping talent and may well get you where you want to go.

First, set aside several hours to be alone. Find a private place which will give you time free of interruption for reflecting and planning. Prepare your list of things that you *don't* have that you would like to achieve. Let your mind run free and do not allow yourself to pause to consider cost, impossibilities, or any other obstacle, logical as the obstacles may be. Give yourself time to develop a list of several hundred items, including the small things as well as the larger, more difficult objects — everything that passes through your mind, from a new pair of shoes to a mansion.

In the final analysis, the things on the list will not be as important as the discoveries you make in *preparing* the list. Also, the list should include things that you want to *become* — tangible as well as intangible. The greatest discovery from the preparation of this list may well be not only what it is that we *want*, but also what we have always wanted to *be* — something that our present occupation does not give us the opportunity to be. Frequently people find themselves deeply entrenched in a profession completely contrary to that which would more properly match their skills or desires, and the preparation of a goal list may possibly reveal that. You may discover, for the first time, that all-consuming obsession to totally commit yourself to a new career that lets you be *you*. As Richard Bach wrote in his masterpiece, *Jonathan Livingston Seagull* —

> **"The most important thing in living is to reach out and touch perfection in that which you most love to do."**

Remember, one of the keys to living the better life is to engage in a profession that you fully enjoy. Otherwise, you find yourself engaging in an occupation out of habit or necessity, rather than something that you deliberately chose to do simply for the joy you receive from doing it. The high financial rewards in life elude those who do not like what they do. Rather, they become an automatic reward, reserved for those whose personally chosen occupation lets them use to the fullest their God-given talent.

The second step for making goals work for you is to prepare a second list, except this list is going to be difficult — painfully negative might be a more proper description. The second list very simply contains all the things you *now have* that you *no longer want*. Here, the challenge will be to force yourself to be totally honest.

Very often, people have trouble developing the first list — things we don't have that we want — because there are too many things in their life that have them turned off. In fact, the human situation can become so hopelessly intolerable that many people just simply give up "wanting anything better" because the futility of their present situation seems to assure that the future will be just about like the past. Therefore, they set no goals because they want to avoid the certain disappointment that will come when they don't achieve them.

As soon as this second list is prepared, we should immediately go to work to eliminate as many things from the list as we possibly can. Sometimes, the achievement of a goal on our first list (or positive list) can lead to the automatic elimination of an item on the second list. For example, our negative list might say "Get rid of my poorly running car that embarrasses me when I drive to work." The first list, or positive list, may contain a goal of rewarding yourself with a new Eldorado. Obviously, getting the Eldorado will solve the problem of having to drive the 1962 Falcon.

Surely, some people will question the value of having a negative list. There are those who believe there is great value in turning your back on thinking any negative thoughts. While there is great value in that philosophy, I have observed that there is greater wisdom in *honesty*. It would be a mistake to emphasize negativity, but occasionally it is wise to be aware of its existence. What we don't know, or choose not to know, *can* hurt us. A lot full of weeds is just that — a lot full of weeds. And the best step toward changing it to an attractive garden spot is to recognize its present status and to then take positive action toward changing it. I firmly believe that "As a man thinketh, so he becomes." Continual thoughts of poverty, loneliness, and dwelling on the negative side of life does in fact assure the continuation of those situations. On the other hand, for every person who emphasizes the negative side of things, there is the would-be-do-gooder who "ho-ho's" his way through life, saying everything is "fantastic," then crosses his legs to expose a hole in his shoe, and later tries to borrow a few dollars for lunch. There is little difference between one who is negative about all positive things and one who is positive about all negative things. One is pessimistic and the other foolish.

Painful as it may be, develop the second list. And then take great joy in checking off items as you slowly, but certainly, eliminate them from inhibiting your better future any longer.

The third step in goal-setting requires that we review our lists each day, checking off the things we have gotten and the things we have gotten rid of. Also, during this daily process of goal review, form the habit of constantly entering new items on your goal list. Finding new things that we want to achieve stimulates the mind in a positive direction, and leads us toward finding the ingredients necessary for the attainment of our goals. Remember always that if the desire for something enters our mind, it means that we also have the ability to get it. The human mind is uniquely designed that way. With the desire also comes the ability to achieve the object of the desire. We may, however, have to work at developing those abilities — possibly because we haven't used them for years.

One of the values that we get from the daily review of our goals comes from *repetition*. The more we review, the more we come to believe that we have a right to *achieve* our goals. Jim Rohn, Chairman of Jim

Rohn Productions, frequently emphasizes that "Repetition is the mother of skill." He teaches that anything repeated long enough will eventually become a part of us — a learned habit — and the daily effort of working with our goals is one of the best habits we can ever learn. When we finally learn to immediately write down a good idea, and word it so that it fits on our list of goals, we are on the road to improving our circumstances massively. Unique ideas and goals — both of which often enter our minds in a flash as if they come out of nowhere — leave us just as quickly unless they are recorded on paper.

A final comment on this third step. Obviously, we should always carry our goal lists with us, either recorded in a daily planner, a journal, or some other book which we carry with us. For years, I wrote goal lists on pieces of loose paper, and either couldn't find the paper (several got washed in the laundry) or they quickly became so worn that their continued use was no longer practical. I would find myself spending more time preparing new lists than working on my goals.

Someone once said that if we go to work on our goals, our goals will then go to work on us. There is great wisdom in that statement. What we "go after" is not as important as what we become. Ultimately, we attract what we are, not what we want, and that finally is the real value that comes from working on our goals every day — what it makes us *become!*

The fourth and final step in goal-setting is called *visualization*. It is the ability to see, hear, feel, smell, and believe yourself to be already in possession of that which you want, or perhaps being that which you want to become. Napoleon Hill's books are filled with stories of individuals who literally "thought" their way into a position, or a better lifestyle. His classic *Think and Grow Rich* has altered hundreds of thousands of lives for the better, including this author's.

Visualization is that remarkable human ability that lets us mentally move into the future — the future of a more happy and productive and prosperous life — and to dwell there momentarily and then return to the present bringing with us the excitement and full belief of what it is going to be like. We can, without cost, visit the car dealership and actually sit in the automobile that we want to have. We can position the six-way power seats, buzz back the moon roof, drop the tilt wheel, pop the automatic trunk release, and then capture the sounds and smells and carry them with us. We can come to know what *that* car is going to be like when we own it. We can also do that for anything else that we want. We can dress the part of what we want to become; we can begin talking, walking, thinking, and in all ways acting as though we already are who we seek to become. Someone once gave me sound advice in a short phrase — "Fake it 'til you make it."

In my own life, I have observed with both curiosity and fascination what I call the *push-pull phenomenon*. It is a major key that must be understood by anyone who is attempting to make goals work for them, rather than working *for* someone else and being a part of *their* goal. Some things are extremely difficult to share or teach, and this is one of those things. I will do my best to describe one of the "indescribable" occurrences that is so important in changing a life, in hopes that you, the reader, will "feel" more than you will "understand." In his book, *Think and Grow Rich*, Napoleon Hill frequently commented on the "secret" buried in the pages of that book — a secret that would jump out at me and reveal itself so forcefully that it would dramatically change my life. When I finished the book, I was certain that I had skipped a page somewhere. Although I was highly affected by the book, I saw no such dramatic idea — and only after years of re-reading did I discover it, for it had to be felt and could not be described. So it is with the *push-pull phenomenon*.

The purpose of going away to a private place and taking the time to write out our extensive goal list is to help us develop or rediscover things that we want — things that will drive us into new activity and rekindle that childish enthusiasm which attracts those events and circumstances that can lead us to a successful and happy lifestyle. The act of forcing ourselves to take the time and make the effort to work out our personal and business goals is what will provide the push part of the *push-pull phenomenon*. Discovering what we want is the first step toward *getting* what we want. Remember — goals have the tendency to *push!*

Now for the difficult part! After we have pushed ourselves through discipline, consistent effort, and constant development and maintenance of our current goal list, we will slowly but assuredly begin feeling a *pull* — an almost magnetic force, or feeling, or attraction. This pull is like an intuitive attraction, a silent voice speaking to us out of nowhere that begins to provide answers and quiet direction to things that previously were "fuzzy" or uncertain in our minds.

Possibly, certain aspects of our goals will puzzle us — our occupation perhaps, does not seem to be the occupation that we feel completely comfortable with, and yet we aren't sure which new course to follow, or what change to make. We find ourselves setting and achieving a few of our goals but the major revelation seems to be missing; the major key that makes all phases of pursuit, occupational involvement, personal confidence, quiet calm — all aspects of our lives — fall quickly into place so that the whole picture of life now finally begins to make sense. This describes somewhat the "pull" factor in setting goals. It is when we find ourselves doing things, saying things, making changes and revising routines, not out of a well planned scheme, but in response to something that seems to be saying "go here, do this, say that, call him, write the note, make the appointment," and hundreds of other little things that by themselves seem to have no real value or to provide any real or immediate benefit.

When we have "pushed" ourselves through executing the discipline of setting goals, the pull factor makes its unique but unannounced appearance, causing us to do things that we do not fully comprehend. The pull factor makes its appearance several times throughout the day through bits of conversation, a passage in a book, an idea out of the blue as we drive down the freeway — even in our dreams it manifests itself, speaking to us, calling, urging, revealing, advising. In bits and pieces it comes, pulling us in a direction somewhat unknown to us. But when we become intelligent enough to respond to "the pull" the bits and pieces seem to inevitably fall into place, almost like the thousand pieces of a jigsaw puzzle being blown by the winds before us, each piece making no sense, and providing no clue as to the part

14

of the big picture that it represents. Then suddenly the wind stops and calm engulfs the area around us; and finally the thousand pieces settle to the ground in front of us arranging themselves into the perfect finished picture of the better life — the picture of ourselves, and of all we have ever wanted to be, and have, and see. This is the difficult to describe "pull." We need only listen, follow, exercise faith, tolerate temporary disappointment, study opportunity, make decisions and selections, and believe in ourselves and the ultimate attainment of that desirable lifestyle which we seek.

Goals provide the "push," and our action, courage, faith, and instinctive human response provides the "pull." The pull is seldom logical, but always present — speaking to us in a silent voice, through feelings, emotions and intuition. We need only to persuade ourselves to listen and to follow in wisdom, confidence and faith. To paraphrase a familiar quotation, we need only to march to the sound of the different (and distant) drummer, however measured or far away. Learn to discipline yourself to create the "push" and become instinctive and intuitive enough to follow the "pull."

Since it is the purpose of this book to attempt to cover all aspects of the goal-setting and achievement process, we also must consider the best answer to the following question:

"Should I tell others about my goal and primary aim in life or do I keep it to myself?"

In reading nearly everything available on the subject, I have found two opposing viewpoints on this question, and while both make sense, here is what seems to work for those who achieve the most. The real power of goal-setting seems to function at its best when we've discovered our long-range goal for what we want to become, and then share it with no one. Remember, here we are talking about what to become, or do: our all-consuming obsession to do something (as an occupation) that will produce all the *things* we want to accumulate. It is best to keep your great ambition within you, for it seems to produce an immeasurable, unseen, inexplainable force which acts as a strong ally in both pushing as well as pulling you toward the actual achievement of the goal. It seems that the more people with whom we share our excitement, the more that excitement becomes diluted. And to further complicate things, we open ourselves to the ridicule and harassment of friends and relatives. When we have "told the world" of our intent, the world will begin to deposit its massive quantities of doubt, pessimism, ridicule and discouragement upon us, and this kind of well-meaning but devastating input will surely take its slow but deadly toll. Our attitude can become affected, our expectancy will diminish, and we will find ourselves having to often defend our announced intentions when the results do not seem to come as quickly as our friends think they should.

Kept inside, goals tend to feed the fires of enthusiasm, confidence and high expectation, until these attributes affect our character, poise, and confidence, and slowly but certainly make us into the kind of person we will have to become to get all the things we want. Difficult as it sometimes is to maintain a shroud of secrecy around our goal list, it seems that we must do exactly that. We all like to boast about the

16

home we will someday have, or the car that will soon be ours, but the best form of boasting is how well we convince ourselves of our intentions. What the rest of the world feels about what we are going to do really doesn't matter anyway. We do not need to impress anyone with our grand intentions. If that is what gives us our kicks, we may discover that we are more serious about impressing friends with boastful but unkept promises than we are with the actual achievement of our goals. Let the achievement of our mighty goals impress others, not the ego trip that some of us like to get from telling other people about our intentions.

While it may sound negative, keep in mind that we won't always get what we want — that seems to be the way the system is set up. Sometimes, in spite of the greatest plan and most sincere intent, we will fall short, or change our minds and decide on something else. When it happens, and you have guarded your goal list and announced it to no one, you won't have any explaining to do. This does *not* mean that we should accept at the outset that setting goals may not work for us — it will work for anyone. But sometimes things happen. And even though we have completely justifiable reasons for not achieving some of our goals, the world will probably not accept our explanation. A good creed to follow in all things (not just goal-setting) is an idea I once heard from Senator Sam Ervin of North Carolina, who advised a colleague, "Don't bother to explain anything to anyone, for two reasons: first, your friends don't require it; and second, your enemies won't believe it."

The concept of "keeping your goals to yourself" is not based upon any scientifically measurable information, nor is it based upon accumulated statistical data. Neither is faith in a creator, or knowledge that wind exists. And certainly no man has, in fact, seen an electron. But all modern technology is based upon certain theory, which when tested and applied, produces certain and predictable results. So it is with the entire procedure of the value and application of setting goals for personal, family, and economic progress. Don't set any, and watch the final results of *that*. The results of that lack of effort are also predictable, and are constantly in view on any street corner of the world.

You now have a basic formula which, when coupled with your own emotion and your own faith, can work miracles for you. One more thing to remember when you apply this formula in your own life is that goals should be as specific as possible. Just wanting a better home or a better automobile is not enough. It seems that the likelihood of achieving a goal is in direct proportion to the ability to see the finer details of that goal.

3

Several years ago, Mr. E. James Rohn presented his *Challenge to Succeed* seminar in a southwestern U.S. city. In attendance that evening was a very young man, barely twenty years old, named Wayne Barnes. The session presented by Mr. Rohn on learning how to set goals was to have a massive effect upon the life of this man. Some time after the seminar, Mr Rohn met Wayne Barnes again, and it was during this meeting that Mr. Barnes showed to Mr. Rohn a model of a home he intended to one day have. He had built the model himself, taking great care to be as specific as possible. The rooms were designed to scale, and in fact were removable. At one point in the conversation, Barnes removed one of the bedrooms in the model home and informed Mr. Rohn that it was to be the guest bedroom, to be used by Mr. Rohn whenever he found himself in town. He also advised Rohn that it was the goals presentation of the earlier seminar that had made it possible for him to have that home, speaking in terms that sounded as though his home already existed. Of course, in his mind it already did. The plans, the faith — the very acceptance of the fact that it did exist — is what finally brought about the actual construction of the finished product fashioned after the small model shown to Mr. Rohn years earlier. That home is today occupied by Mr. Barnes, who credits goal-setting for its very existence.

At this point, a good question might be: "Is it possible to finish something before you start it?" To those persuaded by logic, the answer would certainly be "NO." But to those aware of the magic of setting goals, there is no hesitation in providing an emphatic "YES" to what appears to be a foolish question.

In truth, all that exists was completely finished *before* it was ever started! The home in which I now sit was finished in total detail before construction ever began. Someone, through the ability of his own mind, knew how much wood, wiring, and plaster would be needed; the size of the rooms, the location of the utilities, the design of the Palos Verdes stone fireplace, the height of the matching stone walls surrounding the home. In detail and on paper it was finished before the first shovel of dirt was overturned. The same is true for the two automobiles sitting in the garage — both finished in detail before the assembly line began to roll. What is true for homes, high-rise office buildings, cars, or the massive 747 jumbo jets rolling down the runway is also true for human lives. We can start wherever we are, with whatever we have — or do not have — and with paper and pencil, design in detail exactly what we want to do with what remains of our one life on this spinning planet. Once we capture the magic ability of seeing things that do not exist and going to work to achieve them, we will never again settle for the empty and unchallenging life of letting events and circumstances and someone else decide for us the lifestyle we are to live. If we are able to think, and dream, and want, and plan, and if we are willing to execute our plans through positive human activity, we can and will have whatever we want. Remember, however, there is a major difference between merely wanting, wishing, and hoping, and the unyielding force of intelligently *planning* your better future by applying the laws of setting goals.

The magic of setting personal and business goals comes when we accept with total faith that we are going to achieve them. When we do that, the excitement that comes from that acceptance works its magic and attracts to us the necessary things for achieving the goals. We merely arrange the things, as they come to us, in such a manner as to lead us toward our final objective. In the beginning, we may only have a fraction of the answers we must have in order to reach the ultimate goal. The world is filled with well-meaning but misinformed people who are reluctant to commit themselves to a worthy objective until they have all the elements or ingredients to assure their success — *before* they get started. Their insistence upon assurances or guarantees in advance makes their effort logical rather than emotional, and as a result, the absence of emotion all but cancels their chances for success. It is the individual who embarks on the journey totally committed to "getting there" that meets with success. Even so, his journey toward achievement will not be without the encountering of countless obstacles. His determination, however, allows him to concentrate not upon the encountered obstacle, but upon the desired goal which will make his effort successful. On the other hand, the man who attempts to cautiously plan and reluctantly begin will also meet unexpected obstacles (things he had not counted on) and he will usually be persuaded to give up, turn back, retreat — taking with him his remaining assets, afraid that further delay would cause him to lose everything. Such a person would be wiser never to begin, for he never fully accepted with excitement and belief that his efforts would result in success, and he was therefore doomed to defeat before he began. This does not mean, however, that planning is undesirable; on the contrary, nothing is more powerful than a good idea coupled with a good plan. But the formula should consist of eighty percent idea (and the emotion that accompanies it) and twenty percent planning (the logical mechanical part).

4

Of all the writings and lectures on the subject of setting and achieving goals, none is more important nor capable of bringing about high accomplishment than the knowledge contained in the following simple phrase:

> *"People will always get exactly what they've got to have."*

Most people who read this short message do so without becoming aware of its full meaning. The power that comes to the surface when humans become touched by the extent and accuracy of the above message is phenomenal.

To illustrate the message that humans do, in fact, get what they *must* have, imagine that you, the reader, live in an eastern city. It is January, and the outside temperature is seasonally cold. You are like many Americans: working an eight-hour job, and on a fixed income. You have a few credit cards, and all are very close to being charged to their maximum limit. It is payday, and after work you drive to the bank, make your deposit and go home to write checks to the creditors that you can afford to pay. You go to the supermarket and purchase the food supply for the following two weeks, and after writing a check to pay for that, find yourself with fifty dollars remaining for the big emergencies which may come along before next payday. That evening, with the children finally in bed, you open a can of beer and proceed to position yourself in front of the television set where you will try to escape from the reality of your meager personal and economic situation. Your high point of the weekend will be the weekend sports contest — Sunday afternoon football perhaps. (While this scene may not be typical of your situation, it is definitely typical of several million Americans — those who watch television on the average of six hours daily, and whose lives contain no challenge or opportunity for living a better life.)

Several days later you return from work, and in checking through the mail discover an unexpected but inevitable notice from the power company which informs you that unless you pay the hundred dollars outstanding on your bill by noon tomorrow, your service will be terminated. You may pause to ponder whether or not the power company will actually do such a thing, but experience reminds you that they most definitely will. It does not matter that the temperatures are sub-freezing, your electric power will be terminated by noon tomorrow!

This situation presents a grave problem; you do not have the hundred dollars, and you have no idea where you might get it. You consider the finance company, but you visited there just six months ago, and still owe a balance. You also consider the bank — perhaps a bill consolidation loan (where all your small, difficult to pay bills are merged into one big *impossible* to pay bill), but you haven't paid off the previous note yet. You consider your relatives, even the in-laws, but reject the thought because of the embarrassment that comes from asking again. It is obvious that you simply cannot get the hundred dollars. Even most of the money remaining from the last pay check has been spent on the children's school pictures and a few items overlooked at the super-market. It is obvious that if you could get a hundred dollars you would have it, rather than walking about with a few dollars in your pocket. Your situation appears hopeless.

On the other hand, let's consider the consequences of *not* getting the money to pay the utility bill. Your freezer is going to thaw, and your food is going to spoil. Also, you are going to look foolish running from room to room carrying candles. What will you say if friends drop by during the evening and find candles everywhere? You can try to sell them on being energy conscious, but suppose someone needs to use the bathroom, and you insist that they take a candle instead of turning on the light when they close the door? And, of course, the greatest disaster of all — the television will not work! Imagine trying to get through an evening without television! Probably the most embarrassment will come when you must explain to your family that you, as head of the household, cannot command enough income for your services to pay for the basic essentials. How can your ego possibly face that? Finally, confronted with this dilemma — not having the access to the hundred dollars, and not wanting to experience the chaos that comes with having your electrical power disconnected — you are forced by urgent necessity to take action.

WESTERN IOWA TECH-LIBRARY

What do you suppose the person in these unbearable and apparently unsolvable circumstances will find by noon tomorrow? Right! The hundred dollars! And why did he finally get that which was completely out of the question just a short time before? The answer is found in the quotation — *"Humans will always get exactly what they've got to have!"* And we will always do so, whether we have to get a hundred dollars to pay an electric bill, or a financial fortune. When we *must* do something, we do it. Wishing for it, hoping for it, or dreaming about it will not do it. It is when we are forced into a final sense of urgency that we do those incredible things that were within our power to do all the time.

If this is true, why then, do so many want so much and settle for little? The reason is simple — they don't *have* to have it. They are getting by, and with a slight zone of comfort, humans will coast. Unfortunately, there is only one way to coast, and that is *downhill*, not to the top of the hill. Nature has designed most of us the same way she designed rivers — following the course of least resistance. If we are getting by, we settle for that.

The long range goal which most people share, either consciously or subconsciously, is to become "successful." A good question might be "When does one consider himself a success?" Ask a hundred people that question and you will most likely get a hundred different answers, because success very simply means different things to each of us. Perhaps it would be better if we defined failure and then committed ourselves to avoid our definition of *that*, for the result would then have to be some form of success. Failure could be defined as our inability, for whatever reason, to achieve the goals that we have clearly set for ourselves, whatever they are. Therefore, we could possibly consider ourselves unsuccessful, at best, if we have no clearly defined goals. It is about the same as one who has set goals, and not achieved them. Without a plan — a concise set of objectives with deadlines — we have no means of measuring progress. We consume our years accumulating, pursuing, temporarily enjoying, holding things together, making ends meet, or erroneously accepting a title as a diploma for displaying our success. We raise the children, go through several automobiles, a few homes or a "better" apartment, discard old clothes for new, and manage to feed ourselves fairly well. All of this, however, is not success. It is existence, and many people — if not most —somehow settle for an entire lifetime of existence rather than of substance, and ultimately leave the earth having consumed more than they have contributed, leaving little more than a gravemarker as evidence of their existence.

If we were to place two football teams on a field together, we would assume that a contest among two fairly well prepared teams is about to begin. One "team," however, has only practiced as individuals: some kicked, some passed, others ran, blocked, or just generally "worked out." This team has no integrated game plan, no plays, no team spirit — in fact, none of the members of this team really knows the full objective of the game. This team kicks off to the well prepared team that takes possession of the football, and by using their well planned and executed plays, promptly marches up the field to score. Now the unprepared team has its turn. It remembers the "moves" and general techniques of the opposing team, and now begins its offensive efforts. This team will probably advance a few yards, and then on the advice of someone on the opposition who "feels somewhat sorry" for them, decide to "punt." Once again the prepared team moves smoothly and scores. On the ensuing kickoff, the ill-prepared team once again advances a few yards, appears to be making some progress, but will again (inevitably) punt. And so it goes through the next sixty minutes, with the ultimate final score predictably one-sided.

In this analogy of life, the losing team had "opportunity" each time it had the ball. It made yardage, both on the ground and in the air. Perhaps it even made some first downs. And once, through a miraculous series of incredible circumstances, the team even scored a touchdown. It tried its unprepared best to do what the opposition seemed to be doing, and even appeared to noticeably improve as the game progressed. Had the individuals played for several weeks, possibly they could have become a real team executing and planning their moves with deliberate effort. However, there were only sixty minutes, all of which were used up in learning how "not to do it." Their intentions were honorable, their courage was laudable, but the results were, unfortunately, very predictable.

And so it is with humans. Willing to try, gallant and courageous, trying to learn, making occasional but inevitably futile progress, hopelessly rejoicing over small successes, consuming time with each effort, and finally the game ends — not in sixty minutes, but in sixty years. With goals, game plans, well thought and planned human activity, and conscious practice, life has meaning, substance, lasting rewards, and many times for true rejoicing and relaxation. There is nothing so relaxing as relaxation while winning, and nothing more futile than trying to relax while losing. In the latter case, we find ourselves never fully pausing and resting long enough to renew our strength; and in the former case, each conquest restores and magnifies strength, and provides a confidence that lets us enjoy our times of rest.

Goals make the big difference in how we feel, how deliberately and smoothly we execute, how often we win, how comfortably we relax, how often we laugh and enjoy, and above all else, in how we measure our progress. Without goals there is no measurement, and therefore, no measurable progress.

There is a tendency among people to coast through life honestly believing that their better future is just ahead. Next year will be the year: as soon as the car is paid off, as soon as the next promotion comes, when the income tax refund check comes — these and hundreds of situations like them are empty promises of the future; things we fool ourselves into thinking will change the way life is going for us. This tendency to fool ourselves seems to be quite common. An uncertain future is not quite as intolerable as an unproductive, unhappy present, so we look to the future in hopes that minor changes now will bring about major improvement later.

Here is how the future is going to be — it is going to be just about like the past, until we begin to make major changes in ourselves. This year was probably just about like last year, and next year will be very nearly like this year. The solving of one problem will assure the appearance of a new, unanticipated problem that consumes the meager annual increase in pay which we had hoped would make things different. When we count on small, insignificant quantities of improvement, we find that nature has prepared for us challenges to offset the rewards she gives to us. Only when our massive efforts produce massively greater rewards and results will noticeable improvement occur. This is one more of the reasons for beginning the daily discipline of setting goals — for what it makes us do. Goals tend to push us forward, while a life without goals usually has us being *pulled* forward by other people, often in a direction we do not want to go.

Several years ago, a good friend of mine from Tennessee was encouraging me to go into business with him. At the time, I was in aerospace engineering, and had no business or sales experience. His business proposition required a fairly sizable investment, and since I found myself barely able to pay my bills each month, I was fully against borrowing even more money, in spite of the word picture he painted about how rich we were going to get. I found myself offering my friend the usual excuses for not making such a bold move as he was about to make — my next promotion was just around the corner, things were going fairly well, I didn't want to "rock the boat," and a few others which I have since forgotten. My friend listened politely while I went through my list of reasons for hanging on to my secure position, and why my future was getting better in my present profession. After allowing me to go on for several minutes, he knew that I was trying to convince myself as much as I was trying to convince him, and at last interrupted by asking me a question: "How much money do you have in the bank?" I was so shocked by the question that I gave him an answer. "Forty-eight dollars," I replied angrily. "Reynolds, you've been working for about ten years and you're telling me you've got forty-eight dollars to show for it. That makes you worth about four dollars and eighty cents a year. Now you can stand here and tell me all you want about your future and how much better it's going to be. The truth is, your future is going to be just about like your past. You've got about thirty years left to work and at your present rate, thirty years time four dollars and eighty cents does not make you a wealthy man."

As much as I felt he was discourteous and unnecessarily blunt, I could not argue with the accuracy of his argument. I had been promising my family for years that things were going to get better, and occasionally they did, for brief periods. But somehow the combination of inflation, growing children and infrequent and inadequate pay increases made my general progress curve somewhat horizontal.

Several days later, I resigned my position in aerospace and entered business, and because of that decision, I eventually met the man who was to change my life because of some ideas he shared with me over the years — Mr. Jim Rohn. From him, I first learned of goals and their importance in helping us become more and achieve more. I have learned over the years that human effort, not human ego and excuses, produces a better result. Left to their own direction, people will always do the minimum that it takes to get by, and their reward is a "getting by" result. As I review my own life, I am completely convinced that goals, pursued long enough, planned well enough, and read frequently enough will make the difference between mediocrity and high achievement.

The very beginning of achieving goals is the total acceptance of the fact that you have already achieved them . . .

5

Without question, the individual who plans his own life by setting goals stands a far better chance of living a happy and abundant life than does the person who lets others plan for him. If, in fact, goals do work a magic, and assuming that they will work their magic for anyone who tries — who makes the painful but constant effort to seriously do the work required —then why do so few people ever make the attempt? The why is really not important. The fact is that humans will always act like humans. They will repeat the same mistakes, both of omission and commission, that were made by countless millions who came before them. In spite of the best training by parents (who usually advise us "Don't make the mistakes I've made," or "Don't do as I do, do as I say"), teachers or advisors; and in spite of libraries full of books on the subject of how to become successful, we seem to find unique ways of spending our three-score and ten years on earth, surrounded by opportunity and affluence and still manage to live an empty life, leaving little behind as a reminder that we were here, except for our children who, more often than not, will do just about what we did.

Someone once told me that every effort should be made by every human to leave the earth having given more during our brief stay here than we have taken away, and the failure to do so is the gross misuse of our one life. Imagine what the world would be like if each of us were to discover, develop, and apply our unique individual talents, given at birth, and then based upon our experiences — both the good and the bad — leave behind a book, an idea, a person who our words have touched, or a slightly improved social condition as a result of our contribution during our lifetime. There surely would be little need of heaven, for we would have designed it here on earth.

The excitement of contributing, sharing, discovering, thinking, loving and planning would eliminate the false and temporary excitement provided by alcohol, drugs, and all forms of deception and dishonesty. Perhaps more people do not use goals to plan for more happiness, or more wealth, or more challenge because there are more appealing methods for *temporarily* exciting us that require far less effort and far less pain. For whatever the reasons, the fact is that this book and thousands of others like it contain the very answers which most of us will spend a lifetime searching for, only to discover at an advanced age that the key to our better future has been sleeping deep inside us all those years, while we vainly searched elsewhere. The recognition of this fact, and the commitment to exercise the discipline for changing what we *are* into what we were intended to be, is a most difficult experience for humans to accept and commit themselves to. Personal change is incredibly difficult — possible and probable with enough consistent effort, but difficult and painful. Remaining what we are, and wishing and waiting for things to change is the basic human inclination. It is also a basic human inclination for us to blame others, or to blame circumstances for our lack of progress. Blaming the government, the traffic, the weather, the company, the pay schedule, the taxes, the competition, or the thousands of other wordly circumstances is far more logical and less painful than blaming ourselves. The truth, however, is that what we are, what we have or do not have, is the direct result of our thinking, lack of thinking, erroneous activity, distorted attitude, and developed habits which we have spent a lifetime accumulating, most of which — if we were to be completely honest — are the very source of our difficult circumstances.

The application of goal-setting in our lives takes effort, requires change, discipline, and daily execution and attention, and all of these things are difficult. Therefore, if there is a reason why people do not do better by learning to plan better, this would be it. Personal change is incredibly difficult, but it takes personal change to make goals work. There cannot, however, be any other intelligent choice than to learn to work harder on ourselves than we do anything else, for certainly, in the words of Mr. Jim Rohn:

> *"For things to change, we've got to change."*

What does it take for a person to change? We have all made promises to ourselves in the form of New Year's resolutions either to begin doing this or to stop doing that, only to fall back into the same patterns, and within a few weeks or even a few days we have forgotten that we even made the commitment to change. All of us have said to someone else at one time or another "I'm going to change," and at the time, we were quite serious about it. But more often than not, humans resume their normal behavior, falling quickly into old traps. And later when our repeated errors once again create a new crisis, we re-pledge ourselves to change once more; we re-encounter and solve the problem once more, and once solved, with the pressure gone and the challenge removed, we quietly resume our fairly predictable patterns.

The slow gravitation back to old habits, once a crisis goes away, does not happen suddenly. Our promises and pledges die not in the twinkling of an eye, but very gradually, while we are quite unconscious that it is even happening. In the more elegant words of Bennett, "Ideals die not in the conventional pageantry of honored death, but sorrily and ignobly, while one's head is turned."

Does this mean that humans are destined to constantly repeat deeply learned habits that lead to failure, disappointment, and unhappiness, or is there some magic method for changing ourselves? The answer to both questions is most definitely NO! We are *not* destined to go on as we are, but unfortunately, there is not an easy method for changing what we are to what we would like to become. It is *possible* to do so, but it is certainly not easy.

It seems that humans will ultimately change for one of two reasons. Either inspiration to change, or desperation *demanding* change will move us into new action. But being moved into new action, either by inspiration or desperation, is not enough. Our initial activity — the mere act of taking *action* — will usually provide for us a different result. Simply taking action on a matter will solve or change the *effect;* but the *reasons* (in this case, the person and his behavior and years of accumulated habits) must be totally reversed, or the effect, or problem, will surely recur. So the challenge is to change the *cause* — what we *are* — so that we can expect a better result —what we *get!*

It is generally recognized that the first six years of human life set the thought patterns and form the habits which we will carry with us throughout our entire lives. The habits of lying, procrastinating, sleeping too much, doubting, worrying, shyness and all attributes and liabilities of human nature, did not come at birth. They were learned over a period of years until these habits became at last automatic. And once we instinctively repeat something, be it a physical habit or a mental habit, the mere repetition makes the act even more instinctive. Finally we do in fact evolve not as adults blessed with constant, creative, and constructive habits, but as creatures of instinctive mental and physical responses — repeating past errors, acting without thinking — all of which leads us inevitably to a lifetime of meagerness, emptiness, and unhappiness because we are too lazy to change ourselves, or even worse — *unaware* that our present patterns are inevitably leading us to chaos. Often, we even become angry when someone dares to suggest that we need to change. And, whether our failure to change ourselves is due to laziness, apathy, or stubbornness, the end result is going to be the same. The man sitting on the park bench feeding pigeons because (at age 65) that is all he has to do, will not change his circumstances just because he has finally discovered the reason why it happened. The results of lazy thinking are as disastrous and deadly as the results of procrastination.

True ultimate human destiny is the eternal search for high achievement whether attained or not. This search must forever continue if life is to have real meaning.

6

In observing the actions and attitudes of people around America, I have observed with interest what might be called the "attitude-business cycle." It seems to be applicable to people from many occupational backgrounds, including sales, investments, and politics, and is particularly and most frequently inherent among those who function without specific business and personal goals.

To use an example, imagine a man entering the field of real estate. He is attracted to the profession because of a boom-period in the economy and the stories circulating about the relatively high incomes being earned by many of the sales people, some of whom he knows — people with limited education, little sales experience, and average personalities. As is the case in most sales-oriented careers, it takes time to develop prospective clients, as well as time to learn some of the basic skills necessary for results to appear. While our friend is laying his groundwork and "sowing the seeds," the economy begins to cool off. Interest rates climb, inflation persists, unemployment begins a slow increase. The "prophets of doom" emerge from their cold, dark and conservative corners and begin forecasting recession and other occurrences of economic chaos. Since it is the nature of all things to move constantly from one cycle to another, it is not uncommon for the economy to temporarily cool-down after running hot for a period. After the drought comes the flood; following the intense cold comes the warming spring; after darkness comes the light. To assume that things will stop their inevitable and fairly predictable cycle is foolish.

However, the person in our example is too busy earning a living to adjust to the pattern of all things. Hearing the *news* of coming unfavorable business trends, his attitude becomes affected. Just as he was about to receive the financial fruits of his efforts, he finds his "seeds" eaten by the "birds" of misfortune. Because of his commitment and his need for some kind of meager income, he continues to make a half-hearted effort, making calls without confidence, and making presentations without persuasion. After several months of long days and insignificant results, our friend has finally reached the point where he is ready to give it up and return to the security of a salaried position. As his commitment and daily efforts diminish, the economy begins to show signs of strengthening. Sales in the office slowly increase, and he watches some of his associates begin to receive substantial commissions once again. Since he fears the duration of this business up-turn, he watches carefully while still putting out "feelers" for another position that will pay him what he needs to climb out of his economic rut. Soon, business is booming again, and the prophets of doom crawl back into their cracks, awaiting their next call to action. Finally, our indecisive friend gets re-excited, and once again enters the sales field to plant more seeds. His colleagues, of course, are beginning to harvest their crops, which excites him even more. He spends many months learning, calling, talking, and prospecting — and even makes a few sales. His attitude becomes stronger each day and he talks often now of his own imminent fortune, which is just around the corner. Suddenly, and without warning, the cycle switches once more, and the financial world withdraws, and the trumpets sound as the cracks widen and the prophets once again appear. Our poor friend cannot believe it! Just as his crop was about to come in, the skies opened and hail fell. Predictably, his attitude starts its gradual descent — as does his income.

And so, the cycle repeats itself once again, with human attitude running along at ninety degrees behind the business cycle. Without goals, our attitude is constantly affected by circumstances and when circumstances improve, it takes time for our attitude to correct itself and become conducive to success. With goals, our attitude remains ready for opportunity to present itself, so that when the tide of opportunity rolls in — at predictable intervals — we are mentally ready to ride it as a surfer waits for the big wave, ignoring the calm, and not being tricked into riding the small ones.

A major part of the challenge of doing well is to constantly prepare ourselves in every way with the proper attitude, plan, timing, preparedness, tools, and training, and to do so even when things are not going well, such as when the business cycle is at a low point. It is important to make every effort not to be like our friend, who is neither productive nor ready for productivity — a follower in every way of circumstances, cycles, and other people's opinions, and so very typical of one who has no goals or plans of his own — being affected rather than affecting. By having specific plans and challenging goals, we can spend our time during the winter season of the business cycle refining our technique and developing new skills, and sharpening our attitude so that when the springtime of the business cycle arrives, we will stand ready to take advantage rather than to begin preparing. By waiting for the springtime of the business cycle to arrive before preparing ourselves, we find ourselves ready to sow our seeds not at the beginning of spring, but at the beginning of summer, and come the fall, reaping a meager crop while our associates haul in the bumper crop. At the risk of sounding repetitious, goals alone stand as the one tool available to us all for maintaing our preparedness, so that all elements of our human potential are fully ready to be summoned into total massive action when opportunity presents itself.

7

One of the major purposes of this book is to help all those who read it to reach a clear understanding that a life without direction and specific intent is a life of minor and unplanned achievements. Humans require objectives — something to go for, and when we have goals, we discover talents within ourselves that we did not know we had. We find that the world and all of its obstacles, frustrations, disappointments, and its tolerance for mediocrity will gladly step aside for the person who knows where he is going. An automatic companion of a well directed life is the joy of high productivity. With goals, we seem to convert obstacles into stepping stones, and without goals we engage in frequent periods of self-pity and develop a tolerance for mediocrity. Goals drive us to discipline our disappointments and to become intolerant of those who waste time — either their own or ours. Goals drive us to lead rather than to follow; they drive us to create rather than consume, and to encourage rather than to find fault. Our time is too short to allow ourselves to constantly repeat our own mistakes, or to waste time discussing the errors of others, or to share stories about the evils of the world, or the unfairness of government, or the misuse of tax money. Those who have no constructive plans of their own love to discuss the destructive actions of others;

they remain part of the problems of the world rather than seeking to become part of the solution. Each of us has been blessed with an abundance of talent often waiting to be discovered and converted into profit, happiness, and high personal achievement.

Shortly after I climbed off my mental and financial knees, I found myself swept into a new lifestyle — almost by magic. I had received no "breaks" nor did I sell my soul or principles to anyone. It began one day while I was sitting in the lobby of the South Coast Plaza Hotel in Orange County, California. I noticed a man entering through the revolving door. It was Mr. E. James Rohn, whose *Challenge to Succeed* seminar I had heard in Washington, D.C. many years earlier. Because of that four hour seminar, I had resigned my position in aerospace to enter the sales field, rather than continue in a salaried position in an occupation which I felt did not let me use my natural talent. For several years, I studied and observed people while working very hard on myself. Rohn had said at the seminar: "The major key to your better future is you," and had advised those in attendance that evening to "Work harder on yourself than anything else — including your job." And now, after nearly ten years, this same man whose words had had such a major effect on my life stood before me. I introduced myself and we spent time together that day discussing life, my experiences since that first seminar, and his present intentions to incorporate Jim Rohn Productions and to package films, tapes, workbooks, and workshops into a marketable service for the general public. It had been one of my dreams since first hearing Jim Rohn to one day work for him, and shortly after this second meeting I joined his new company as a salesman. After nearly a year of expanding the company throughout California, I decided it was time that I moved into a new area with Mr. Rohn's company. I began scheduling myself into service clubs and various associations as a guest speaker, doing very much what Rohn himself does. In fact, I saw myself as a direct assistant to Rohn, and even went to the extent to have new business cards printed, with my title shown as "Special Assistant to the Chairman of the Board" — which of course was not true, since such a position did not exist.

In my mind, the position *did* exist, and I had long visualized myself filling it. Within a few months, I was promoted to be Jim Rohn's personal representative and my duties were to go where Mr. Rohn could not go, and to say what he would say. Also, one of my new responsibilities was to conduct the prestigious *Leadership Seminar* as a full participant along with Rohn. My long range goal, set nearly ten years earlier, had been achieved. I was teaching goal-setting with the man who had first introduced me to goals many years before — at a time in my life when I would be one of the least likely candidates ever to do such a thing.

Looking back over the ten year period (from where and what I was) to my present situation (where I am and what I am), one thing stands out as being of significant importance. My goal was not so much to work for Rohn and to do what he does as it was to become the *kind of person* it would take to do what he does. *That* is one of the keys to getting whatever one desires —not to achieve a position or a level of income, but to visualize the kind of person we would have to *be* and to then go to work on *ourselves* to *become* that kind of person. The skills, knowledge, breaks, and all other things and events necessary for the achievement of the goal will then automatically gravitate to us over a period of time. The formula becomes simple — find an idea that seizes your imagination and allows you to use your best skills; couple that idea with faith and constant daily effort and the passage of enough time, and you will emerge one day exactly into the life situation you had planned. Along the way, however, expect discouragement, doubt, and periods of disgust. You will often be tempted to abandon your effort in the face of massive discouragement. On occasion, the facts of reality will leave you with no choice other than to give up on your ambition and settle for that which you are lucky to have. But remember — when we consider ourselves lucky to have what we have, we almost automatically become unlucky enough to get anything better. Gratitude is a good human characteristic, but not when we use it as a crutch for not trying to improve ourselves. Resigning ourselves to "being grateful for what we have" is a virtue, provided we do not spend what remains of a lifetime just being grateful.

8

Shortly after becoming Mr. Rohn's representative, I was scheduled to deliver a series of seminars in South Africa. One of my assignments was to present the entire two-day, twenty-hour *Leadership Seminar*, without E. James Rohn — I would not only cover my material, but his as well. When advised of this responsibility, the staff of Jim Rohn Productions expected that I would be shocked, or afraid of possibly being unprepared. Instead, I can recall only feelings of massive joy and total confidence, for in my mind, I had already performed that assignment a thousand times. So it is with challenge and achievement. If we believe in an idea or undertaking strongly enough, we frequently see ourselves doing that which will one day certainly occur, so that when the opportunity arrives we need not prepare, only perform — usually with brilliance and perfection.

On that trip to South Africa, I sat next to a young man during the flight from New York City to Rio de Janeiro. We discussed business as well as people. The purpose of his trip was to "find himself." He intended to live on the few hundred dollars he had with him —to hitchhike, work odd jobs, sleep on the ground, and simply do whatever necessary until he found his great ambition. He was from wealthy parents, and against their wishes, decided that he did not want to finish the few hours necessary to graduate from college. During the conversation, he asked a very interesting question — three words that later caused me several hours of self-examination to answer. His question was — "Are you successful?" I recall telling him that his question was not an easy one to answer. If I were to consider only the opportunities I now had, the answer would certainly be "yes." But, if I were to consider whether or not I had achieved all that I wanted to do, or all that I wanted to become, or whether I had become all that I was intended to be, the answer would most emphatically become "NO." We all pursue "success" — I know of no one who plans to fail. So if we pursue this condition called success, how will we know when we have achieved it?

The young man left the plane in South America without an answer. I spent the next ten hours en route to Johannesburg, South Africa, pondering his question and making notes in my journal, and from those hours of deliberation and introspection emerged with what has since become part of one of my seminars. I delivered it for the first time to a couple of hundred business men in the city of Johannesburg where it was incredibly well received — not because I delivered it or because the thoughts and words are mine, but because it helps to answer the question "What is success?"

I call it the *Five Keys For Becoming Successful*, and the following briefly describes those five inseparably connected keys.

PERSONAL SUCCESS — Jim Rohn once said to me: "People don't attract that which they want, they attract that which they are." Becoming a better person provides for us the automatically better lifestyle, and becoming a better person is not all that difficult. We can make a conscious daily effort to work on the little things such as our handshake, smile, our walk, the words we use and how we use them, the way we dress, and a thousand other little things that make us what we are. And make no mistake about it— what we have (or do not have) is a direct result of what we are or of what we have allowed ourselves to become over the years through a gradual and certain accumulation of habits, both physical and mental.

Much of what we are is a direct result of what we think of ourselves. What we wear is a result of how we think of ourselves, and if we think poorly of ourselves, either consciously or subconsciously, it will nearly always show up in how we dress. And remember —neither success, successful people, nor opportunity come to those who appear unsuccessful. It has been said that "success attracts success," and how often have we heard that "The rich get richer and..."

Truly, the self-image we have is the first of the five keys for it directly affects the other four.

The key phrase to remember in becoming "personally successful" is —

Learn to love yourself *first!*

This sounds rather selfish and egotistical. I do not mean that kind of self-love that makes us feel that we are better than other people. Such a feeling can be self-destructive. It is good to feel that you do not have to look up to, or down on, any other human being, and it begins with loving — and liking — yourself first.

A woman asked me, "Do you mean I should love myself more than my husband?"

The answer is "Absolutely!"

She then said, "Well, certainly you don't mean that I should love myself more than my children."

The answer to that is "Definitely!"

Too many people labor under the misconception that we should sacrifice our own happiness for others. I have tried that, and it is foolish. The one very best favor we can do for those we love is to work harder on ourselves than we do on anything else. How often I have heard a man or a woman say "I'm keeping the marriage together for the sake of the children." How totally foolish! An unhappy marriage and an unhappy family are the results of unhappy individuals who live together. If everyone would learn to do what is necessary to like *themselves*, they would automatically solve their problems. And if you are close to someone who insists on *not* liking themselves, then extract yourself from being around that person — they will kill you!

Learning to like — or love — ourselves is really not a violation of any community ordinance, marital vow, or spiritual law, and yet some people think there is something terribly wrong with it.

Unless they have rewritten it again lately, the Bible still instructs — "Love your neighbor as you love yourself." The very obvious suggestion is that it is quite normal to love yourself! How can we possibly love others when we don't even understand the meaning of the word as it applies to us? How can I possibly give love to someone else when I don't have it for myself? You cannot give that which you do not have. I may say the words "I love you" to someone else — perhaps because it is expected of me, or because it seems to be what is said in a given situation. But I cannot truly give the "deep inside emotion" that goes with those words unless I know of their deepest meaning for myself in my own private self-world.

There appears to be a direct relationship between goals and self-image. Those whose lives are directed by the intense "push" of personal and business goals seem to be consumed by an intense belief in their ability to achieve them. Their confidence soars and their self-image escalates. They become directed more toward thoughts and conversation on the subject of achievement than on worrying over obstacles, or the fear of failure, or gossip. With goals, and the proper self-image, obstacles become stepping stones toward achievement. With each accomplishment comes increased confidence, clearer plans, and constant and courageous effort.

It is unimportant whether setting goals increases self-image or whether working on improving self-image triggers goals. Discussion on whether the chicken preceeded the egg is folly. The fact is, both exist! For me, the self-discipline for setting goals and getting excited about pulling future excitement into the present did something to my feelings about myself. My past failures were no longer important and I stopped worrying about what other people would think about me if I did things that seemed to be pretentious. The poor and the unambitious will do what they have always done — they will laugh at those who try to get ahead and they will find fault with those who have already made it. They will blame others for their horizontal social condition. Someday, one at a time, a few will make the greatest change humans can ever make — they will simply change their *minds* about what they are willing to accept. They will recognize their right to excel, and go to work on themselves. When that day comes, they will discover that success is really easy — we need only to want it, and then to feel that we deserve it.

Perhaps that is as good of a success formula as will ever exist, so if you missed it:

First, you must want something. (DESIRE)

Second, you must believe you deserve it. (SELF-IMAGE)

Third, you must plan to get it. (GOALS)

Fourth, you must believe you have it. (FAITH)

Finally, you must put your plans to work. (ACTION)

If there is a weak link in the achievement chain, it is most likely the last step. Too many people have taken Napoleon Hill's best-selling book title too literally. You do not simply *Think and Grow Rich*. I know of one person who has read that book for seven years, but has never taken action on his lofty thoughts. He professes to have goals, he reads the books, but his own *personal* growth and image of himself are on the critical list.

Without question, personal success — what we are, and what we appear to be — is the first step to actually becoming and having more.

OCCUPATIONAL SUCCESS — The second area of our life that needs attention is the thing we do to earn an income. Some people call it a "job," others refer to it as a "position," "occupation," or "profession." Whatever we choose to call it, we have got to enjoy it and do it well if it is going to be a source of great reward. For each of us, our occupation is either a blessing or a curse. Based on personal experience, I have found that if I looked at what I did as a "job," it usually was just that. It turned out to be a place where I worked just hard enough so that I didn't get fired, and my employer paid me just enough to keep me from quitting.

For our lives to be complete, to make life fully worthwhile, we must find the occupation that lets us use most of our abilities. Remember the unique quotation from *Jonathan Livingston Seagull:* "The most important thing in living is to reach out and touch perfection in that which we most love to do." It would be wonderful if more people would arrange their lives to do that. No doubt the divorce rate, crime rate, and drug use rate would all diminish if everyone were "occupationally content."

One of the greatest benefits I have received from setting my personal goals was the final discovery of what I *really* wanted to do. I knew that aerospace engineering was not the answer after several months in the industry. I soon reached the same conclusion after selling life insurance, wigs, soap, memberships in a boat-owners' association, burglar alarms, and exercise machines. Each product, each opportunity, had made others rich, but I lacked that secret "something" that turns mediocre performers into champions. I knew for years that the "thing" I always wanted to do was teach — to share ideas, and to touch people with words. It seemed to be my natural talent. I had difficulty finding an opportunity that paid people to simply "talk to others." Finally, after attending a seminar in Washington, D.C., I made the discovery that there were those earning incomes doing just that. There was one problem, however. The desire to "speak" must be coupled with a unique ability to speak. The man conducting that seminar gave me the key on how to do it.

Jim Rohn said, "To attract more, become more."

He also said, "To get a better position with a better future, become a better person."

There was the key! I had the desire, and I possessed some of the ability. What I needed to work on was *me*.

I remember Rohn saying to me, "You've taken thirty-two years to get yourself going in the wrong direction, so don't expect me to change it in thirty-two minutes of conversation, or thirty-two hours, or even that many weeks. But if you want things to get better for you, you've got to begin today and be willing to make a conscious daily effort to change."

I have now worked on myself for over ten years —not just to earn more, but because I want to grow more, and be more, and share more. I have learned that what we give out does in fact come back to us, in much greater quantity. So I will continue to do all I can to learn more of how to share ideas that affect people in a positive way.

And so, because I have found the thing that gives me occupational success, I find I can put everything into what I do. I can watch a movie or a show on television, and find things in the conversations, actions, and results of other people that add to my storehouse of information. My thoughts are on my profession, either directly or indirectly, when I drive my car, sit alone, or converse with a friend.

Whether you are an engineer, a salesman, a homemaker, or a laborer, you can fully enjoy what you do. Don't worry about the money — whatever you do, if you do it well, and do it long enough, you will find yourself one day earning more than those around you who just "do it for a living." As I've heard Rohn say, "Your talent will create a place for you." Begin small, if necessary. Make "wages" or finge benefits secondary to full, honest, and enthusiastic performance.

Sometimes we can find both income and opportunity for personal growth by participating in sales-oriented companies that allow us to work part-time. I am asked to speak quite often to companies that offer attractive incomes on a part-time basis. But the greatest benefit of participation in such companies is that they offer some of the finest personal development and training programs available. Their best advantage is not in what they help us earn, but rather in what they help us *become*. Some of the companies I have been most impressed with are Amway, Princess House, Shaklee and a few others that offer that blend of excellent products with unique opportunity. I know of several people who have started in some of these companies to earn supplemental incomes, and — because of what they learned — became rather wealthy. Some go on to full-time participation in those companies, and others go away and carve out their fortunes in careers they had never before considered, simply by putting to use what they learned while earning — and learning — on a part-time basis.

Reading books is an excellent way of discovering our untapped abilities. The libraries are full of books on how to live a better life. The problem is, the libraries are not full of people. Recently I learned that less than three percent of Americans have library cards. The answers lie waiting in books, waiting to be opened and read by people — but the people are too busy watching television and earning a living to take the time and effort to tap the treasure waiting to be discovered on the printed page.

I have often wondered why people read newspapers but won't read books like *The Greatest Salesman in the World* by Og Mandino. Newpapers tell us how bad it is. Books tell us how good it can become, and yet we elect to read the things that discourage and limit our enthusiasm and spirit. With some of the things I've seen people read, even a bullet to the brain would be no less deadly!

FAMILY SUCCESS — The third part of our life that affects whether we become successful or not deals with our private world. Whether we are married, single, divorced or just "going together" with someone, each of us has someone who affects us — who feeds emotional input into our mental factory; someone whose daily words and actions determine how we feel. Here is the key element to remember on the subject of "family success:"

Everything affects everything else!

That statement may sound like a trite expression, and its full impact may easily escape us, but we must be constantly aware of its truth. The person who leaves home in the morning free of emotional turbulence and content with the fact that all is well at home can fully direct his or her mental energies in the business world toward plans, goals, and activities that will reap a heavy financial harvest. When a marriage is a union of two happy, patient, and understanding people, the love that created the marriage continues to grow and to give even more reasons —or goals — for doing well in the business world.

One of the greatest forms of living hell is to live in a marriage that limits our individual quest for high achievement. Where jealousy, impatience, temperamental accusations, and poor communication exist, success cannot. We find ourselves on an emotional elevator ride: having a few good days, getting momentum going in the business world and then through a foolish word, impatient act, or unwarranted verbal attack we slip backwards, falling victim to hurt feelings because our spouse — for whatever reasons — chose to say or do things which took their toll. Many marriages exist exactly this way. The spirit of understanding, harmony, and mental and physical attraction which created the love seems to have quietly slipped away. In its place, we find ourselves legally bound to someone who limits us —or so it seems. The truth is, that *someone else does not limit us; we choose to limit ourselves.* When the fire of marriage has given way to the smoldering ashes of discontent, it is the fault of two people whose failure to understand and accept well-meaning advice has led to a marriage of bodies rather than a marriage of minds. The fact is that the truth of any issue nearly always lies somewhere between the two extremes of the issue. A marriage, and its associated happiness, dies when two people slowly but certainly fail to see the other side.

I do not have the training to give "authoritative" advice on marital problems. I have observed the slow undoing of my own marriage and I am aware of the consequences of an unhappy, deteriorating relationship on the business side of life. Trying to do well in the market place while our family struggles in unhappiness is destined to end in disaster. I am aware of one particular marriage which continues to this day when it should have ended years ago. It remains "legally alive," and the two continue to exist with their children simply because of shame that would surely come from their church and their relatives were they to end it all. One of the parties to this marriage told me of her private hell many years ago, and insists that the marriage continues only for "the sake of the children." My last advice to the woman was that she should do the one best favor she could possibly do for the children, herself, and her husband, and that is to end the foolish pretense. It seems that when the emotional fire has gone out of a relationship, it can never again be rekindled. Counselors will counsel, ministers will administer, and friends and relatives will advise, but when it's over, it's over!

To repeat — *everything affects everything else.*

Blessed is the one whose marriage continues as one

of the world's great love affairs, for it will feed the fuel of emotion into the market place, and profits and progress will grow as the world feels the mighty effects of love and harmony in the home. What I am, I am because of those who touch my life each day. And if I am touched by anger, impatience, and dissent, the results will show up on my financial balance sheet.

Let's take a short word journey into an early morning segment in the life of an American family. John, the husband and father, wakes at 7 a.m. and dresses for work. It is Tuesday, and the work week is not yet half over, though it seems like it should be Friday. The weather is as dreary as his attitude. He remembers that today is his turn to drive in the car pool, so he quickens his pace.

John rushes downstairs and into the kitchen where he is greeted by a familiar scene. His children are having their breakfast (they've been up since six, focusing in on test patterns in preparation for a day of television viewing) and his wife is moving from refrigerator to stove and back again. Seeing him enter the kitchen, she apologetically advises him that the kids have eaten the last of the eggs, and that he will have to settle for toast and coffee. With the words barely spoken, he watches as the toaster belches its black smoke upward — and as his young son points at the coffee boiling over, he spills his glass of milk. John rushes to unplug the toaster and steps on bits of cereal which missed the bowl sometime earlier.

In anger, John makes his first comment to his admiring family. "I hope this place looks better tonight than it does right now!"

With that, he slides on one sleeve of his worn jacket and moves toward the door. Noticing his planned exit, his daughter makes her first comment —

"Daddy, I need five dollars for class pictures today."

"Get it from your mother. I'm running late."

His son gives a slightly subdued "Good-bye Dad," and John, with his feelings hurt and ego over-inflated, doesn't even bother to respond. The awareness that he doesn't have the five dollars until payday on Friday is almost more than he can handle, and he hopes that perhaps his wife will have a few dollars stored away for emergencies.

As John opens the door, his wife glances in his direction, hoping that he will at least look back so their eyes will briefly touch — at least she will know of his feeling in spite of his childish behavior. Instead, he closes the door and walks toward his 1962 Falcon station wagon. Seconds later, backing through a cloud of blue smoke, John is on his way.

One hour later, John rolls into the office parking lot even more unnerved at the incompetent drivers and poorly synchronized traffic lights, pondering the atrocities, muggings, accidents, and announcement of increased interest rates — all heard on twenty-four hour action news which he listens to each morning on the way to work. He climbs out of the car and mutters an insincere "Have a good day" to his passengers. His temper quickly jumps as he notices the recently promoted assistant manager walking into the building. It was the promotion he thought was rightfully his.

As he approaches the door to his office, he notices several associates standing inside, a few of whom notice him. As he opens the door and steps inside, he plasters on an artificial smile as if to say "My world is in good shape." With that, he will now enter into eight hours of affecting the public with the depth of his wisdom, sincerity, and genius.

Who's kidding who?

Remember, everything affects everything else! We cannot separate our private world from our business world, and what we are in the private world ultimately and certainly determines what we get from our business efforts. Somehow, it shows up in the things we say, or the look on our face when we think that no one is looking. We can wish for things to get better, and wait for the promotion to come through, but until we become the kind of person who deserves the better condition or position, we will always have what we now have; or put another way, if we don't become more than we now are, we will always have what we now have. For things to change for John, John has got to change.

One of the best things that John could do for his family would be to go to work on setting goals. A sincere and honest conversation with his wife would be a good beginning. The admission that his lack of progress and short temper is the result of self-dissatisfaction will be painful, but it is also necessary. Such a conversation could well re-ignite the feelings that existed before the love affair became a marriage, and give John the "shot" that he needs to create family and individual objectives. He may well find things that the members of his family want that he wasn't even aware of, which give him reasons to make new efforts and to show a new excitement. Once again, there will be reasons for conversation, for now there are common goals to pursue.

Family goals are the best assurances of family happiness! When individual family members become excited and happy, the family automatically benefits, for the word "family" merely describes a group of individuals with a common bond.

> *Learn the wisdom of accepting criticism from someone who cares for you, or one day you may find yourself forced to accept it from someone or some experience that does not care.*

> *Love is the acceptance of a person for what they are — and for what they are not.*

> *I will promise to work on me — for you, if you will promise to work on you — for me...*

SPIRITUAL SUCCESS — The fourth key is one which must be examined briefly, and no effort will be made here to persuade the reader towards any religious view. It is my wish only to suggest that most of us have in the past, and will in the future, call upon some supreme being or outside, non-terrestrial source for counsel or guidance. Usually, such appeals — perhaps a prayer — come only in times of great human tragedy, and are uttered by atheists and agnostics, as well as the religious.

Since religious inclinations are a very personal matter, I will only say that all of us need to turn outside of ourselves for answers on occasion —

toward whatever source of answers we happen to believe in. For those who profess to believe in a creator of all things, we must communicate with that source often — not just in times of crisis. To profess a belief in God, and to fail in doing our duty to that God, whether in the form of prayer, scriptural reading, church attendance, or paying a tithe, is neglectful, and we will pay the price in a haunting guilt which will adversely affect our productivity in the market place.

Many years ago, I was given a simple phrase which combines the pursuit of goals with religion, and which provides unlimited promise to all mankind. Its message summarizes all that this book attempts to do, and reveals to all who accept it that the destiny of all humans is to reach ultimate perfection. To reach a true understanding of the magnitude of promise that this phrase offers is the key toward the attainment of any goal.

> *"As man is, God once was — and as God is, man can become."*

My own personal conviction is that we all came from somewhere — our existence did not begin at birth, nor did the existence of humans begin with something crawling out of the swamps and standing erect. We are here for a purpose, and after life on this earth, I accept the promise of an after-life. While we are here, we each are given the responsibility to grow and prosper. We are given talent as a gift at birth, and each of our talents are different, and each set of talents — if used — are all that we need to become materialistically and personally and spiritually wealthy. We are also given what I call "free-agency," which lets us decide to use, misuse, or ignore our talents and abilities. We are sent here, in my judgement, to magnify our calling, and to improve ourselves in every way, and to satisfy the law of eternal progression that governs all things. The choice is ours and yet many do not know that a choice exists. We continue to be content with a fraction of the achievements which we could have. We cease to grow and learn. We lose our sense of urgency. We exchange our unlimited, immeasurable human potential for mediocrity, or a title, or a salary, or a bottle. We forget that "What we don't use we lose," and finally our talents become rusty, neglected, or even remain undiscovered. I do not know enough of religious philosophy to supply answers, counsel, or advice. I cannot describe God because I have not seen him. I do, however, believe in myself and in the potential of all people. I accept the value of goals in helping us become all that we were intended to be. I believe that without goals in our lives, humans become little more than robots.

As someone once said several thousand years ago:

"Without a vision, people perish."

Spiritual success — let each of us find it in our own way; but when we find it, let us have the wisdom to keep it alive and functioning as one of the five keys.

ECONOMIC SUCCESS — The final key to the achievement of a successful life is one which many seem to consider the most important part. For me, it is the least important on a list of things to be pursued, because in studying the lives of both the successful and the unsuccessful, it is my opinion that money —in quantities that make life comfortable — comes as an automatic result of doing other things first. It seems that to pursue money is to assure that it will not be acquired. The pursuit of money is like chasing a rainbow — when we get to where we think it is, it always seems to be somewhere else.

Here is an important comment which many must learn to accept if true economic security is ever to be attained:

"Having money is not an indicator of success, nor is not having money an indicator of failure."

I am acquainted with many people who are doing quite well financially, but whose personal lives lie in ruin at their feet. Their children are constantly having problems, their marital relationship is unhappy beneath the surface, and their business is controlling them! But if you were to ask most of them if they were "successful," they would sit back, smile and say, "Yes, life has been very good to me!" I have often wondered how it is that the accumulation of large amounts of money or property is automatically associated with success. Many people give up on wanting to be successful because of what it seems to have done to some of their friends.

Let one thing be clearly understood by all who read these words — money has no power to either create or destroy human character. Money is merely a symbol — a piece of paper. What *humans* do with it, or for it, causes problems, however. Blaming money, or the lack of money, for problems is like blaming television for crime among young people. If there is something on television that is detrimental to the mind, a human decision coupled with a human act can result in the switch being turned off to eliminate the source of negative input. Instead, we complain about it but continue to watch it. How foolish! I have often heard it said that "money will only make you more of what you already are." If we tend to drink excessively, having lots of money will only serve to permit us to drink more and better.

My decision to make economic success last among the "five keys" does not mean that I am suggesting it is not important. On a list of priorities, however, it is least important when compared with other things. But the attainment of the first four keys without some success at becoming economically secure is dangerous if not impossible. It takes economic security to make any — or all — of the first keys work well, although many people will disagree with that. Some claim to be happy even though they are broke. I used to do that, and I did it to make myself feel better. There is nothing pleasant about poverty, and to labor under the pretense that because our friends are broke, it is all right for us to be broke is a deadly and unforgivable human error.

Looking back into early years, I can recall being taught by my grandmother that "in order to be humble, you've got to be poor!" There were the early scriptures that I was taught to memorize, such as "Money is the root of all evil," and "It is easier for a camel to pass through the eye of a needle than for a rich man to enter the kingdom of heaven." It was those erroneous and misinterpreted teachings that, at an early age, formed my opinion that to do well was to do wrong. Each of us are already all that we need to be in order to get all that we want and all that we deserve. It was mentioned earlier, however, that most of us fail to reach our full potential because we never really discover what we want, and when we reach only an average level of performance we settle for that and then convince ourselves that we are happy with what we have and that "more" would only corrupt us anyway.

It is, in my opinion, the natural human destiny to achieve all in life that our God-given talent would, if used effectively, permit us to achieve, and to settle for less is to fail in life. At best, we will have existed but will certainly not have succeeded, and the day will surely come when we will be held accountable for that — either to ourselves, our family, or our God.

In reviewing the *Five Keys to Becoming Successful*, it is apparent that to fail in any of the five is likely to have a massive effect upon the other four. We must exercise daily care to make certain that each of the five parts of "success" are in order, or our success may become partial, temporary, or both.

There are certain basic laws governing nature as well as mankind, which if understood and used can lead us quickly and surely toward whatever form of achievement we desire. The basic law covered by this book is that "people will always get exactly what they *must* have," and a *goal* is merely a condition, position, or item that we *must* have. Setting goals and working with them on a daily basis provides us with enough emotional reasons for taking positive and massive action. And remember, with enough *reasons*, people will do the most remarkable things. Without sufficient reasons, people will do average things, normal things, mediocre things, and there can be little joy in being average. Average is OK, but if we can *get* and *become* more, who wants to be average? Someone once said that "average is the best of the worst, and the worst of the best." It seems that when people resign themselves to the limited happiness that being average provides, they have — at that moment — died!

As surely as seed will grow better in more fertile ground, so will the application of setting goals work better in some situations than others. It would be foolish to assume that "setting goals" will always produce an equal result for anyone who uses them. The medicine that cures one will poison another.

For goals to *really* work — to get the full advantage of changing your life for the better through the development of business and personal goals — it is necessary to make the following comment:

"As long as we are willing to continue working for someone else, we are going to receive only a fraction of what we are really worth."

In the ten year period that I spent being employed and receiving a fixed salary, I observed that, more often than not, my best efforts went largely unnoticed and unrewarded. Promotions and salary increases were usually given in accordance with seniority, or as a result of union demands, and seldom in recognition of talent and ability. It seemed that everyone in my department was called into the supervisor's office at about the same time each year, and given approximately the same increase in pay. I cannot honestly say that those pay increases were commensurate with performance. Those whose effort, contribution, and loyalty were in question received raises along with those whose effort, contribution, and loyalty were beyond question. There were, of course, rare exceptions; but rare exceptions included those who received undeserved rewards as well as those whose rewards were fully deserved.

Mastering the magic of setting and achieving goals provides the greatest results when in an occupation where uncommon effort and contribution are automatically recognized and automatically rewarded. The field of sales, for example, allows people to effect their *own* income by making more sales. If our goals drive us to new and higher levels of sales, our income is immediately increased, since it is tied to a percentage of the sales volume. The person whose sales commission is ten percent will raise his or her own pay by getting ten percent of ten thousand dollars in weekly sales volume rather than the ten percent of five thousand produced the week before. When employed by a corporation that pays us a fixed salary regardless of common or uncommon effort, our next paycheck will still be the same amount. In sales, if we desire a higher income we need only remember that our "next raise becomes effective as soon as *we* do." Of course, if we produce nothing in a particular week, we receive nothing. In essence, we can get rich, or we can go broke — in accordance with our own confidence in our ability to produce results!

Setting worthy goals can result in failure if we merely sit back and wait for someone else to reward us for our effort. We can generate new excitement, new ambition, and produce new results, but if our superior is insensitive, incompetent, or greedy, we may find that others receive recognition and rewards, and we receive nothing. If that happens, we may give up on goal-setting, and make the judgement that they simply don't work — which of course would be an erroneous judgement. If I were to sow my seeds on the concrete freeways of Los Angeles during the spring, I could hardly expect a crop of corn come the fall. It does not mean that my "empty crop" was because of poor seeds, nor does it mean that seeds do not produce crops. It *does* mean that there is a *place* for sowing seeds. In the fall, I will surely find a few stalks of corn growing along the soil-lined edges of the freeway, but not the bounteous crop that I would have had if I had sown my seeds in an area more conducive to success.

Earlier, I commented that "as long as we are willing to work for someone else, we are going to receive a fraction of what we are really worth." In some circles, that statement will be unpopular, but often that which is true is also unpopular. I have worked for two major corporations and studied many more, and in most cases I have observed the same system at work. Companies will employ accountants, laborers, secretaries, engineers, technicians, and will pay a fair "wage" for each to apply their individual skills for producing the collective corporate result. At the end of that year, the profits produced by the application of talents and skills of the employees will be divided not among the employees who produced those profits, but among a group of investors or stockholders, whose direct efforts had nothing to do with the success of the corporation. The employees receive only token pay increases, usually not even enough to keep up with the increase in living costs. Pay increases may, for example, amount to five percent, while inflation is seven percent. The employees are getting two percent poorer every year, and working fifty weeks out of each year. They are told when to work, what to do, when to take coffee breaks, and are even told when they may eat lunch. As long as they are willing to accept those limitations and restrictions, they will be paid every other Friday. Is it any wonder that employee theft is high, or that "sick-pay" continues to be paid in constantly increasing amounts —often to those who were only "sick of going to work?" Should we wonder why coffee breaks take thirty instead of ten minutes, or why product quality control is a never-ending difficulty?

Obviously, the employer-employee relationship is part of the American system. It cannot and should not be changed, for each of us is free to break free of our employer and to become his competitor, and to become an employer of others who have not yet developed the courage or confidence to leave the ranks of those who will settle for the security of a salary. Fortunately, only a handful of people of any generation will ever seek to become independent of any employer. The masses will accept their security, be grateful for it, and die with it. That just happens to be the way people are. A million will read this book out of the two hundred million who *could* read it, and of the million who read, only a fraction will respond with positive human activity. Such does not make this book a failure — it does, however, make humans quite predictable, and such predictability makes life both interesting and disappointing.

I once gave a speech to a college fraternity comprised of young men and women studying administration. One of the respected alumni of that fraternity, who also addressed the gathering, was an employee/executive of a large corporation. In his remarks to the young people who valued his experience and advice he said, "Remember, you can only succeed in life if others want you to succeed." How terribly tragic that this man had traded his excitement of earlier years for such an empty personal philosophy. How even more tragic that he allowed himself to feed such limiting, unchallenging, and erroneous judgements into the mental factories of those who still have hope and hunger for adventure and high personal achievement. For those whose lives are uninspired with the continued quest for attainment, and who have no ambitious goals, such is the level of their thinking.

To those who read *these* pages, let one thing emerge with clarity. Regardless of your age, or present circumstances in life, allow yourself to accept employment only for as long as is necessary for you to formulate your personal plan for living the better life. Force yourself if necessary to impose rigid demands upon yourself, for surely no one else will do it for you. Your goals must be a product of your own desires and decisions. Your activity in the pursuit of those goals must be exerted with consistency, confidence and faith, and tempered with compassion. Surely, no other person is going to care — not enough to get you to do what you should be willing to do for yourself. Your employer is not going to give you *his* position. It is unfortunate that people will usually "give " only as it best serves their better interest, and that kind of "giving" is of little value. In the final analysis, the world — and perhaps even our God — will care for us only in proportion to how much we care for ourselves, and the magic of setting goals can provide the initial spark that ignites the fires of human desire and self-respect.

Let goals help you discover, within and for yourself, the excitement that comes with living the life that truly allows you to become all that you were intended to be.

True succcess is not something that is achieved; rather, it is something that is pursued — a series of accomplishments mixed with failure that make the present better than the past, and the future full of high anticipation and excitement.

9

I mentioned earlier that one of the lessons I have learned from Jim Rohn in the years I have known him is that everything affects everything else. All that we do, think, and experience has an effect on all other parts of our life. Dissention at home affects our productivity in the business world, and the disappointments of today strengthen our character to bring about the assurance of a successful tomorrow. And so it is with goals. The act of setting and pursuing them will surely affect what we are, how we do things, and what we become. We must be consciously aware of what we become in the pursuit of what we want, for surely our efforts in achieving goals are going to change us, and changing ourselves affects those around us. In turn, if our change is negatively affecting those close to us, especially our family, dissention arises, and the dissent and disagreement then affect our attitude. Since our attitude is very closely linked to the size and scope of our goals, we will find that our goals will be adversely affected by the appearance of dissent.

Therefore, the caution light should come on when we find our pursuit of goals affecting our individual and family happiness. After observing thousands of people who make goal-setting and achievement a part of their lives, my conclusion is that the involvement of families working together on their individual and collective goals produces the best results. It occasionally happens that we find ourselves in such intense pursuit of goals — status, things, recognition, and power — that we sometimes lose control of priorities. When we commenced our journey into new directions, commitments, and achievement, we did so for certain reasons. There were things and people that were important to us, and possibly we committed ourselves to a better life not only for ourselves, but for those we loved. If that was one of the primary reasons for our original commitment to excellence, then it is most important that we remind ourselves each day of not only what we want, but also of why we want it, and who we want it for. Failing to do this, our ultimate discovery could be the attainment of many (or even more) of our goals, but the loss of those for whom we pursued those goals. It has well been said by those speaking with wisdom and inspiration — "What profit a man to gain the whole world and lose his own soul?"

In my own life, I have fallen victim to this very real problem. It seems that it is a constant companion of achievement. For every loss an eventual gain, and for each gain an ultimate loss. This should not, however, discourage any of us from planning as well as achieving a better life. By using wisdom, diligence, patience and understanding; and by implementing sound principles in time management, maintaining priorities, and full family involvement, the losses suffered need never even approach the victories gained. Through neglect, carelessness, impatience, and the lack of personal development, the losses can, however, be staggering, making the over-all effort not worth the price paid. It is essential that we make absolutely certain that our personal development grows to keep pace with our achievement, or eventually our achievements will surely shrink back down to match what we are. Our character, poise, personality, charisma, ability to uniquely communicate, and our awareness and sensitivity to life and people — these and all other desirable attributes of human nature — must be constantly developed along with our bank account and general list of worldly achievements. The failure to do so may result in our achieving much, but becoming less, and the great loss from such a needless consequence could become the loss of our love for our spouse and the ultimate break up of that foundation of happiness — the family entity.

It bears repeating one more time — *beware of what you allow yourself to become in the pursuit of what you want.* The happiness and peace of mind from successfully meeting this challenge is immeasurable. The loneliness, disappointment and undesirable grief from failing to meet the same challenge is a taste of hell.

In the words of E. James Rohn, "Better to share a unique love with someone and live in a tent, than to dwell in a mansion remembering only the loss of that one great love." Having paid the heavy price of losing my family through neglecting the garden of my marriage, I feel I can speak out with some degree of practical experience on the subject of what it takes to keep a marriage happy so that the celebration of goal achievement can be enjoyed by a family who pursued those goals together — who succeeded as well as failed together.

Occasionally, people who hear my story at seminars, workshops, and speeches are somewhat misled into assuming that because of my mistakes leading to the loss of my marriage, I now lead a lonely and unhappy personal life, and that all those who experience similar losses are doomed to a lifetime of emptiness, guilt, and regret. This is fortunately not the case. Remember, for every loss there is a gain; or in the words of Napoleon Hill, "Every adversity carries with it the seed of an equivalent or greater benefit." No tragedy of life should ever be allowed to erase the following opportunities and rewards in life. Our decision to mentally cling to feelings of guilt or anger or similar negative memories do, however, cause us to do just that. All people who experience personal difficulties should remember that it is also a time to grow and to add to the memory bank of experiences which will build character and strengthen our resolve.

In my own life, I have discovered that the two darkest years of my life have also served as one of the best training programs I have ever experienced. There is in every human loss or failure, an equal measure of potential good for every measure of human pain as a result of that loss or failure. There are two things that must occur for the good to display itself — the passage of time and the concurrent development of a proper attitude. All that man is comes through the process of his own thinking habits. Forever clinging to a negative experience assures the continuance of emotions from that experience. Think guilt, attract further guilt; think poverty, attract more poverty. And so it is with all of the negative human emotions such as failure, timidity, suspicion, jealously, envy, and greed. I am no longer lonely because I was convinced that a blessing would ultimately gravitate to me and replace my loss, as surely it did. Because of my loss I was to be led to someone who would help me to see the best in myself, so that I would finally purge my personality and thinking habits of those thoughts and deeds which brought about that very loss. I am now totally convinced that the loss was necessary for me to realize my mistakes of omission as well as commission. The same mistakes made with regard to my family were affecting my business life as well. Because of the years of accumulated habits which began at birth, I found myself instinctively responding to challenges in my business affairs in the same unpredictable and ineffective way that I responded to the challenges of serving as head of the family. It took that massive negative experience of personal loss for me to become serious about setting goals, using my talents, and planning for my own life rather than being content with others planning my life for me.

It is now impossible for me to return to the past and rekindle the love, respect, loyalty, and total togetherness which I once experienced with my family. The opportunity was once there, and through neglect the opportunity is now gone. It has been replaced with a new set of opportunities, challenges, and emotions. My doubt has given way to confidence, my reliance upon others has fallen under my expanding self-reliance, and my empty and unpatterned existence has seceded to a life of personally selected goals and ambitions. None of these changes or achievements would have occurred without the deep emotional shock which I ex- perienced earlier.

Be constantly aware that from every challenge emerges opportunity; from each setting of the sun there follows a sunrise; from each loss, a gain; and from each winter, a spring. All life — all nature — is delicately balanced, and harmony is the destiny of all things. Be grateful for adversity, for it is the seed of tomorrow's great harvest — of the blossoming of your full potential; for the opportunity for the emergence of your natural personality and destiny.

10

One of the more difficult lessons to learn is that we should not wait for emergencies to drive us into action. We should learn to drive ourselves toward high accomplishment, toward the attainment of worthy objectives. Instead, through neglect, laziness (in thinking as well as action) and complacency, we allow circumstances to deteriorate until action is no longer just advisable, but mandatory.

The accomplished Dr. Julius Erving — "Dr. J.," as he is called by his pro-basketball teammates — once commented that one of the keys to his incredible success is that he constantly demands more of himself than anyone else can demand of him. This is the mark of professionals, both in the world of sports as well as in the world of business, or in the world of life. Our friends, relatives, and business associates will allow us to get by with so very little. Only when we individually want something with an insatiable passion will we move into relentless activity.

For our own good, we must — if we are ever to rise above mediocrity — push ourselves. The world is usually too busy looking after its own affairs to take the time to do those things which are designed to help *us*. Only on rare occasions does someone *else* enter our lives who pauses long enough and cares genuinely enough to spend time enough to get through to us the message of urgency. If we wait for someone else to enter our lives, we could discover that we waited too long. We could well find ourselves like the man in a small boat, two hundred feet from Niagara Falls, with no motor and no oars. For him, it is too late — it is over. He can do nothing more than sit in the temporary safety of his little boat and wait for the inevitable consequences. It does no good to panic when the falls are fast coming into view. Trying to paddle to the far shore with his hands, or calling out for help is now futile. The key effort to avoid such a hopeless situation would have been for the man to have mentally pictured this terrible scene two miles upstream — while there was still time to do something about it. But two miles upstream, the waters were calm, and the sun was warm, and it seemed it would always be that way. The bystanders on the far shores all noticed the man slowly drifting by, but all assumed he knew what he was doing. And finally, delay, lack of attention, and the mistaken assumption of others took its deadly toll.

The message here is simple. In your life, wherever you now are, however it may be going for you, take the time to become aware. Listen for the sounds up ahead. Set your goals. Find out what you want, write it down, and review it every day. And also, make a list of things that you *don't* want, and go to work on that list, too. Find out what turns you on and work hard at doing well at it. Learn to put everything you've got into everything you do. Learn to want things — whatever they may be — with an all-consuming obsession, and then, and probably *only* then, will life begin to turn a new, fresher, more rewarding direction. Want something! Force yourself into "having to do it or die."

There can be no question about it; the individual, in order to excel in his personal life, must have personal goals which are clearly defined and which drive him forward. Without goals, the individual staggers aimlessly through life, achieving that which occurs by accident, having no means by which to measure his performance other than to compare himself to the relative progress (or lack of it) made by his neighbors and business associates.

Nations, being comprised of individuals, must also have their goals — supported by enough emotional reasons — if they are to flourish. A nation without goals, without leadership by both example as well as inspiration, flounders in pools of doubt and self-pity. Elected leadership, at both the local and national level, must inspire others to exert every effort, use every talent, to bring about personal accomplishment and enhance national pride. It is not the role of government, however, to legislate personal goals — that responsibility rests with each of us. This much is for certain: without inspiration and reasons for setting goals and striving to attain them, the individual effort is not total. Instead, half-hearted efforts are made, confidence gives way to doubt, pride succumbs to shame, and welfare rolls increase, unemployment rises, and disunity threatens to break down the very walls of the democratic structure. Recall, if you will, the national effort in putting the United States first in the space race. The news media followed every step — offices and factories were filled with radios tuned to the latest news on developments — it was a time of great national pride. Being American was to be among the blessed of the earth.

Recession gave way to prosperity during that era, and individual rights and personal accomplishments were the standard.

We now, however, live in a different age, brought about by our individual and collective attitudes about ourselves, our government, and our future. But as it has been over the last 6,000 years of recorded history, this nation is merely the collection of 220 million attitudes, dreams, and ideals. As our individual attitudes deteriorate, so does the national attitude. As we look about us, we find reasons to quit, rather than to proceed, we find reasons to condemn rather than to encourage. In spite of it all, however, the potential for massive human accomplishment thrives, for all that need be done to change our national direction is for us to change our individual minds. And as it took years for us to lose national direction, so it will also take time to redirect ourselves to follow new ideals, to pursue lofty challenges, and achieve mighty things, both individually as well as collectively.

I once met with a civic organization, at lunch, that took nearly thirty minutes to raise thirty-five dollars. The goal was attained —finally — but only amid feelings that reduced grown men, without *large* goals, to beggars; the complaining, the bringing up of irrelevant analogies, the dissent — all were having a contagious effect. Better the goal had been $35,000, at least the mental and vocal hassle would have been worth the effort. Challenge yourselves to reach, to aspire, and to achieve beyond that which is routine. As one man once said, "Set big goals, because small ones have no magic to stir men's blood." Another writer said, "Better to aim my spear at the moon and strike an eagle, than to aim at the eagle and strike only the ground." Perform with such zeal, achieve so greatly, that your associates from afar seek after you that they might share in and learn from your unique accomplishments. Put everything you've got — individually and collectively — into everything you do.

Anyone can produce an average result — the whole world is "getting by." Nine out of ten Americans, in the most affluent society in the history of mankind, are "getting by." Challenge yourselves with adventure. Think, act, speak, smile, dress, produce, plan, create, pray, organize, and manage with an enthusiasm, a zeal, and a determination that causes the world to move aside and those around you to be affected by your momentum.

Have a profound, positive effect upon one another, and in so doing, your organization will prosper, your pride in yourselves will abound, and your contribution toward local and national progress will be massive. Others will seek to emulate your example, and the resultant effect on those around you will be awesome — the effect will set off a chain reaction which will be felt throughout the community which you serve and will reach beyond your wildest dreams. Make your effort worth your while!

Recession always comes, but with regularity it is followed with prosperity. We are inspired by our national and local leaders, and we are dissappointed. We have drought, followed by rain in abundance. The parched and dust-blown field of today reaps a massive harvest next year. Smiles are replaced with tears. After defeat comes victory, after dusk comes the dawn. Bathe in the personal recognition you receive today, for tomorrow you sit silently and unnoticed, while the acclaim once reserved for you is bestowed upon another — who before, sat alone, and watched you.

Let the dead bury the dead. But for those of us who live, and plan, and create let us carry on with living our lives to the fullest — let us create so massively that the world seeks to do as we have done. These things, and more, we can accomplish when we but change our minds and set our goals.

The journey toward any worthy goal is accompanied by uncertainty as well as confidence; failure as well as achievement; and days of disappointment intermingled with days of pride.

True character is developed not in the absence of problems, but in our response to them.

We cannot blame either our character or our accomplishments on circumstances any more than we can blame the mirror for how we look.

*Each human achievement opens
new doors to previously unthought-of
plans and goals.*

*The difference between wanting
and wishing is massive.*

The full awareness of the unlimited human potential lies in the promise that - "As man is, God once was, and as God is, man can become."

*More important that "aquiring" is
"becoming". What we become will
finally attract all that we want.*

For further information on:

Audio Cassette Programs
Videotape Training Programs
Advanced Leadership Programs (public and private)
    Time Management
    Personal and Company Game Plans
    The Magic of Business and Personal Goals
    Personal Development
    The Characteristics of Leadership
    The Art of Communicating
    The Effect of Family on Individual Performance
Personal Development Seminars
Sales Seminars and Sales Training
Guest Speaker Services
Individualized Workshops
Custom Designed Seminar, Videocassette and Audiocassette
    Tape Programs for Corporations

Call or write:

Discovery Publications
22951 Mill Creek Drive
Laguna Hills, CA 92653
(714) 951-7874